A DIFFERENT DRUMMER

to Jerry
If this is better than the
draft you read, you get the
credit.
Thanks
    Gerry

My Life as a Peacetime Soldier
Gerard Teachman

For more information about this title or to order other books
and/or electronic media, contact the publisher:

Atkins & Greenspan Writing
TwoSistersWriting.com
18530 Mack Avenue, Suite 166
Grosse Pointe Farms, MI 48236
www.atkinsgreenspan.com

ISBN
978-1-956879-13-1 (Hardcover)
978-1-956879-12-4 (Paperback)
978-1-956879-14-8 (eBook)

Printed in the United States of America

Cover and Interior design: Van-garde Imagery

Dedication

THIS BOOK IS DEDICATED to the memory of my parents, George and Ebba Teachman. The Gerry Teachman who enlisted in the Army in 1957 and was discharged in 1960 was essentially a reflection of them. My father often said:

"You can raise a child to age twelve, from thirteen to sixteen, offer strong advice, and from then on, all you can do is pray."

It was my mother who did most of the raising. She read a few of the popular child-rearing books and decided that there were only two essential rules: the first was, if an infant is crying, there must be a reason. The second was that all children need someone who gives them unconditional love, and she gave me that throughout her life.

My father offered most of the strong advice, and when I reached thirteen, it was up to my mother to do the praying. My father was an agnostic. He probably just knocked on wood and hoped for the best.

I am profoundly indebted to both of them.

Our daughter, Valarie, was in a terrible car accident on March 9, 2022. She passed away nine days later. She read all of my drafts and her comments and insights enhanced each one, which gives this book special meaning to her mother and me.

Contents

Acknowledgments

I want to thank: my wife, Mary Jean; my sons, Robert and Jonathan; and my daughter, Valarie, for reading this book at various stages. They corrected numerous errors and offered useful advice. I also want to thank my Army buddies, especially Bob McCall, for fact-checking my memory, and for offering candid comments and encouragement.

I want to thank a number of friends who read my drafts and made candid and constructive comments. Ron Lloyd, Lew Loren, and Mike Connor are childhood friends who epitomize all that is so extraordinary about "old friends."

Pete Warner is an Army buddy. I first met Jerry Rozanski in college after the Army. I met Bob Berg fifty years ago and he immediately became an old friend. Ray Ingram and John and Kay Golden are new friends whom I had the pleasure of getting to know better through a book club at Turtle Creek Golf Club.

I want to offer a special thanks to Jill Kramer and Elizabeth Ann Atkins, my two editors, for their expertise and their kind encouragement.

Thanks, again, to all of you.

Prologue

Technically, I'm a veteran. I joined the Army on June 26, 1957, and I was honorably discharged three years later. However, when I'm in the presence of veterans who served in wars, I remain silent. On Fourth of July or Memorial Day celebrations, veterans are often asked to stand up when they're in certain situations, and I do. However, I always feel a little bit like a fraud. Combat veterans make important sacrifices while they serve. Some lose parts of their bodies. Some die. And some return physically whole, but are forever emotionally changed by their experiences, which helps explain why they almost never talk about the war to their families or other civilians.

My experiences in the Army were extremely different from those who served during wartime. The time I served represents three of the most rewarding years of my life, and, strangely enough, three of the years when I felt the most free. Don't get me wrong, the Army owned me twenty-four hours a day for those three years, and they never let me forget it. I was a GI, which stands for "Government Issue." I even found out when I was stationed in Monterey, California, that if I got sunburned on the beach, I could be charged with damaging government property. I really never got used to the idea that even my body was owned by the government.

The Army took a nineteen-year-old, inexperienced teenager and turned him into a twenty-two-year-old young man who was a bit more mature, much more worldly, and a little wiser. Although the Army owned my body, they only cared about where I was and what I was doing when I was supposed to be on duty. When I was off duty, I could do nothing or anything, and as long as I reported back to duty on time, I was free. Some soldiers made very little use of their freedom, but I reveled in it.

During the two years I was stationed in Germany, I traveled as far south as Spain and Italy, and as far north as Sweden and Norway. I went as far west as I could in France and traveled to London, but I was limited in terms of my eastern travels, because of the Communist borders of Czechoslovakia and East Germany. The farthest east I went was Vienna.

My experiences in the Army were exciting and always strangely edifying. I learned a great deal—much of it the hard way. I was put on restriction a few times, which is called an Article 15, and I was put up for a court martial once, but that was later dismissed.

Joining the Army was probably the first real decision I ever made. My life beforehand consisted of living where my parents did and generally doing what they wanted me to do. I was extremely unhappy when they moved out of Detroit into one of its suburbs, but there was nothing I could do about it, except complain. I was fifteen years old, and not ready to live up to my threat of leaving home.

I got good grades through elementary school, but in junior high, I discovered girls, and my grades slipped a bit. In high school, I did just enough to graduate. I even got accepted into college, which my parents expected me to do, but this came as a big surprise to most of my other relatives.

I was going to call this book, *A Diary of a Peacetime Soldier*. It reads like a diary, because it's a first-person narrative, and it's chronological, but that title would be misleading. The events I describe all happened more than sixty years ago. I never kept a diary while I was in the Army, but I did save every letter I received, and I kept in touch with a number of my Army buddies, including Bob McCall, my high school friend who enlisted with me back in 1957.

Conversations with my pals and the letters I still have reminded me of incidents and helped in the chronology. However, I rely mainly on my memory for these stories. Considering the unreliability of memories, this book may well be classified as a work of fiction, but I promise you—the reader—that everything I recount is, in my mind, truthful, and is as vivid to me now as when it first occurred. In a strange way, it's not as if I'm remembering incidents in my life; it's more like I'm having new experiences that in some mystical fashion seem familiar.

There's an important aspect of my life in the Army that I need to explain. There was compulsory military service in 1957. Every boy registered for the draft at eighteen years old, and if you were drafted, you served in the Army for two years. The other services did not draft. Enlistment in the Navy, Marines, or Air Force was for four years, and if you enlisted in the Army, it was a three-year commitment.

Enlisted men in the Army often served with draftees who never let the enlistees forget that they volunteered. They figured that if you enlisted, you asked for it and had no right to complain.

I never heard a draftee say that serving his country was a noble thing or something that filled him with pride. Instead, the prevalent thinking was that military service was an obligation without a choice. Many young men tried to bypass this obligation, and some succeeded, especially the sons of the connected. The draftee's main goal was to make the best of a bad deal. Men who were draftees almost never volunteered for anything. They were seldom motivated, which meant that they didn't try to be the best they could be. I'm convinced that during wartime, that attitude changed, but in peacetime, draftees were counting the days until their two-year obligations were completed.

I enlisted, but I had a draftee's attitude. I wanted training that I could use. I agreed to give the Army an extra year in order to get a better deal, which I was led to believe was guaranteed. I found out that I was misinformed, but with some perseverance on my part and a great deal of luck, the Army provided me with a six-month course in German at the Army Language School, which translated into a major in German and twenty college credits.

CHAPTER 1

Basic Training

Fort Leonard Wood, Missouri

I joined the Army on June 26, 1957. I wanted to go into the Army straight out of high school in January 1956, but I couldn't find anyone who would go with me, and I was a little leery about going by myself. I asked my friend Bob if he'd go, but he wanted to attend college. I don't think it was his thirst for knowledge that motivated him, but rather the idea of a certain amount of independence and the availability of an abundance of young females.

Starting that fall of 1956, the two of us went to Wayne State University. We joined a fraternity, which was really a glorified drinking club filled with interesting guys, most of whom were Korean War veterans. We enrolled in five classes each semester.

At the end of the first semester, Bob and I were doing about C+ work in most of our classes. During the second semester, however, Bob's attendance became less and less frequent, as did mine, but not to the same degree. By the end of the second semester, it was painfully obvious to both of us that we weren't ready for college.

Bob suggested that we join the Army, but I acted as if I were no longer interested. I told my friend he had to give me a good reason to enlist, especially after all the trouble and harassment we went through while adjusting to college and pledging our fraternity. He said he would, and, uncharacteristically, also said that he'd buy me dinner at an expensive restaurant we both liked, but seldom could afford.

He did some research, and after our steak dinner, he told me that we could join the Army Security Agency (ASA). He said by doing so, we would make ourselves eligible for the Army Language School. When we got out of the Army, we could use our courses at the Language School for one year's college credit. I waited until after ordering an expensive dessert, and then I told him I was sold. The next day, we joined the Army.

Our recruiting sergeant was a good actor. I didn't realize how good, until I found out that much of what he promised us was untrue. In describing the ASA, he first pulled the shades down on all the windows and the door. In a conspiratorial whisper, he told us that he wasn't allowed to reveal too much about the Agency, but he could tell us that if there *was* a war, we would know about it before the president did.

He then asked us a few preliminary questions to make sure we could qualify for a top secret security clearance, which was necessary if we were going to be in the ASA. He said the first thing that would disqualify us was if we weren't native-born Americans. I told him that I could trace my ancestry back to the Revolutionary War.

He then asked me, "Which side?"

I thought that was pretty funny.

He sent us to have physical examinations. First, they measured and weighed us. Bob measured a little over 5'11" tall. I measured a little under that height, thereby forever putting to rest our argument over who was taller.

I was definitely thinner, though. In fact, I was skinny. I weighed 133 pounds, and Bob weighed about fifteen or twenty pounds more than I did. He'd always been athletic and played football and basketball throughout high school. When he was twelve years old, he won a statewide ping pong championship for his age group. I played sports from the time I was young, until the time I discovered the opposite sex, which was when I was about fourteen years old. I was also fairly confident that I was never going to play for the Detroit Lions or Tigers.

After we left the physical exams, we were both given copies of the results. My report said that I was in acceptable physical condition, which surprised me a bit, because I'm colorblind. They did give us eye exams, but they had nothing to do with color. They said I suffered from "pes planus, 3° bilateral." I had no idea what that meant, and neither did Bob.

His physical exam was also good, except for a notation that he suffered from mild "dorsal kyphosis." We went home and hurriedly looked up both those terms. Whatever they meant, we assumed they couldn't be lethal, because the Army said we had to report for induction the next day. But we were still curious. My diagnosis meant that I had flat feet, and Bob's meant that he had slightly stooped shoulders. I thought the Army wouldn't take someone who was colorblind or had flat feet. But apparently, I was once again misinformed.

Bob and I left Fort Wayne Recruitment Center in Detroit on June 26, 1957, after being sworn into the Army along with seventeen others. We were driven to the local depot, where we boarded a train to Fort Leonard Wood, Missouri. During the train ride, we got to know the other guys. A group of us played dice, probably because we'd seen too many Abbott and Costello movies. As I recall, Bob and I both won, which was a good start.

The first thing I noticed about Fort Leonard Wood was the humidity. We arrived about 4:00 in the afternoon, and within an hour, we were all damp—and we stayed damp. They marched us to a large, wooden building and issued each of us a fatigue shirt. We then went to the mess hall and ate our first Army meal, which wasn't too bad. Afterward, we were told to report to a barracks, where we were each assigned a bunk, two sheets, a pillow, a pillowcase, and a blanket. The sergeant then came in and issued each of us a white towel. As he was leaving, he randomly picked six of us and told us to wrap our towels over the ends of our beds. Someone asked him why, and he said it was to inform the sergeant who would be on duty the next morning that we had KP (kitchen police) duty.

At 5:30 a.m., the sergeant came by and not so politely awakened the six of us who'd been chosen, which included both Bob and me. We stumbled over to the mess hall on what was already a very humid day. I soon learned that saying "a very humid summer day" in Fort Leonard Wood was extremely redundant.

The mess sergeant assigned each of us a task. Bob had dining room duty, and I was given the back sink. The cook told me that my job was to clean all the pots and pans. I asked him where the soap was, and he handed me a bar of Fels Naptha and a large, empty fruit can with holes in the bottom and a wire across the top. He said I was to put the soap in the can and hang the can over the hot water faucet. I was then to turn on the hot water, which would run over the bar of soap and create all the suds I needed to wash the pans. He was mistaken. The breakfast pans weren't much of a problem, but they served meatloaf at lunch, which was very greasy.

I ran the hot water over that seemingly insoluble bar of Fels Naptha soap for what seemed like forever and never produced sufficient suds. Each time I'd finish scrubbing a pan and rinsing it, I'd run my fingers over the bottom of the pan, and it felt like it was covered with Vaseline. I didn't know exactly what that mess sergeant would do to me, but I didn't think he was going to be happy, and he wasn't. I had to wash each of those pans about six times.

We weren't issued boots, so I was wearing a pair of loafers that very quickly became soaked in grease and hot, slightly soapy water. We were in this mess hall from 5:45 in the morning until 8:30 in the evening. The six of us were then told to return to our barracks.

On the way back there, a sergeant stopped us and told us he needed help with putting storm windows away for the summer. Apparently, Fort Leonard Wood was just as uncomfortable in the winter as it was in the summer, when it went from hot and humid to wet and freezing. We each lugged about six heavy storm windows from a truck down to the basement of a barracks and stacked them against a wall.

When we finally got back to the barracks, it was almost 10:00 p.m. Bob threw himself onto his cot, looked at me, and announced, "I joined the Army to learn how to appreciate my home, and I do. Lesson learned. Let's go home. I want to go home."

We looked at each other and silently counted the number of days before that would happen.

That next day after breakfast, which was acceptable, we joined a long line of newly arrived recruits. Our first stop was to get our hair cut. All of us could be identified by our haircuts at that time. Those who'd gone to college had shorter hair, either a Princeton or a brush cut. Even I had short hair. After I started college, I left my hoodlum uniform and hairstyle behind me. The boys from the farming areas had conventional haircuts with parts on the left side of their heads and little waves in the front. The hoodlums had longer hair with ducktails in the back and longer sideburns. By the time the Army barbers were through with us, we all looked alike.

Our next stop was to get the rest of our clothing. While going through the line, a young man who looked more timid and out of place than any of the rest of us inserted himself between Bob and me. We found out that his name was Frankie. He was a brilliant student, but socially a little awkward and uncomfortable. We were all a little apprehensive about our new lives as soldiers, but Frankie was close to terrified.

We were each given three khaki dress shirts and told to put one on. Frankie tried to put his on over his head without unbuttoning the buttons. That didn't work. I watched him become more and more entangled in his new Army shirt. The pleading look on his face was like a drowning puppy. I told him to stand still, and I unbuttoned the shirt, which he was then able to put on. Now he looked at me like a puppy that had just been rescued from a raging river.

Bob and I didn't know it then, but we'd been adopted by Frankie as his surrogate parents, or better said, his guardians. I don't know why he picked us. Maybe we looked friendlier than the others. Or maybe he just took a chance and hoped and prayed that we'd treat him well and protect him from those who wouldn't.

We all took our newly issued Army gear back to our barracks. Our sergeant showed us how we were to hang up our wardrobes on a little rack behind each bunk bed, and how to store the rest in a footlocker that was at the end of each bed. He also showed us how we were to make our beds, Army-style. It took a while for each of us to get settled and a lot longer for Frankie, but eventually, we looked like a typical bunch of recruits.

This was a time when the Army offered the option of joining the military for six months, and then five and a half years of the National Guard, including monthly weekend meetings and two weeks of duty each summer. Fort Leonard Wood, Missouri, was the recruitment center for a number of midwestern states, and even though it was quite a large fort, we were soon inundated with new, six-month recruits.

The Army has a rule that I think was probably introduced in the time of Caesar: recruits are never allowed to sit around, even if there's nothing to do. We started our eight-week Basic Training course with what was known as "zero week." During that time, recruits go through Army orientation and are introduced to what lies ahead. Our battalion consisted entirely of enlisted men, so the Army didn't feel the same sense of urgency that they felt toward the six-monthers. We started and finished zero week three times. At the end of each stint, they'd send us over to a temporary barracks and bring in a new bunch of six-monthers. Since there was the "no sitting around" rule, any sergeant could grab a few of us to do some "slave labor," usually picking up papers and trash around the different areas, which the Army for some reason calls "policing the area." Or they'd assign us to KP. The rest of the guys were given other busy work.

Fort Leonard Wood has a rocky terrain, along with its extreme climate. One day, four sergeants came to get the rest of us "slaves" and lined us up, single file, on either side of a long, gravel road that led somewhere. We were told to pick up the largest rocks in the road and put them in a truck. The problem was, there was only one truck, which drove slowly down the middle of the road. We picked up and threw one rock into the truck, then waited about fifteen minutes for the truck to come back. We did this for the rest of the day. I believe that I rid Fort Leonard Wood of eighteen rocks that day.

One day after breakfast, we were in formation on the field near our barracks. The sergeant ordered all college graduates to take two steps forward. He then ordered those with three years of college to also step forward. Then those with any college at all were ordered to step forward. Bob and I were in the last group.

He then said, "I want all you college guys to police the area. That means pick up any butts or trash you see. In the meantime, I want all you dumb sons of bitches to watch the college guys; maybe you can learn something."

There was a group of noncommissioned officers (NCOs) and a couple of officers standing by who watched this and enjoyed it tremendously.

The next time I was assigned to KP, I attempted to strike a deal with the sergeant in charge. Six other recruits and I were working in the mess hall on a Sunday, which we were told was always a slow day. We were supposed to be there until 8:00 p.m., but I asked the sergeant if we finished before eight o'clock, could we leave? He told me we could. I passed the word to the other six guys, and we finished at 7:00. I told the sergeant we were finished, and we were ready to leave.

He said, "I'm afraid not. The Army says you're here to 8:00. If I let you go early, I could get in trouble."

I wanted to ask him why he'd lied to us, but I decided not to. I simply learned another lesson about the Army.

Before Bob and I joined the Army, a fraternity brother of ours who'd been a Marine during the Korean War told us that the Army couldn't legally court-martial someone until they'd been instructed in the Uniform Code of Military Justice. This hadn't happened to us yet, so Bob and I felt we could take some chances.

After they would take us out of zero week to start a new zero week a few days later, the Army rule of no standing around kicked in, and most of us were assigned to mess hall duty. Bob and I both had had enough of that, so when they marched seven of us over to a mess hall and told us to sign in, Bob signed a fictitious name, and so did I. We then walked out another door, knowing that the mess sergeants wouldn't assign duties for about a half hour. We also knew that the mess sergeants never knew exactly how many men were being sent to them. After leaving the mess hall, we headed for the nearest safe haven.

Fort Leonard Wood was (and still is) a huge fort, and many of the soldiers there, who were assigned to other schools and other duties, were classified as "permanent party." All soldiers looked alike to the casual observer, and recruits had nothing on their uniforms to identify them as recruits. Bob and I would usually find what the Army called a day room, which was a large room that contained pool tables, chairs, and racks with old magazines. We spent the day shooting pool, something we probably did too many times in our civilian life. We ate lunch in the cafeteria and went back to our area about dinnertime. We didn't get caught, so we decided to push our luck. After the fourth time we did this, at the end of the day, we returned to our area and saw a group of our friends who seemed to be waiting for us. They didn't look happy. They told us they resented us bugging out of duty, and they were going to teach us a lesson.

In our group was an older guy who'd been in the Navy, was discharged, and decided to re-enlist in the Army. His name was Tom, and he was about 24 years old. He asked the spokesman of the group, "Are you working any harder because these two guys are gone?"

The spokesman answered, "No, but it's not fair that we have to work, and they don't."

Tom said, "You don't have to work either, if you're willing to take the risk they're taking. If they get caught, they'll be in a shit-load of trouble. So why get pissed at them, just because they're willing to take the chance and you're not?"

I don't know what they would have done if Tom hadn't stepped in, but I was grateful he did, and I thanked him. The three of us became good friends and got into our share of trouble all through our time together. Tom taught us a lot about how the game was played.

☆ ☆ ☆

One Saturday afternoon, the sergeant marched us over to one of Fort Leonard Wood's movie theaters. I've always loved movies. My father didn't like going into theaters, because he was uncomfortable in crowds, but my mother adored films. She started taking me with her when I was about eight years old. When we reached the theater, I assumed we'd be dismissed and allowed to go to a show like normal people, maybe even be given a chance to buy some popcorn and a box of Milk Duds. Instead, we had to march into the show single file and stand in front of our seats until ordered to sit down.

I thought, *The Army's even trying to ruin my childhood memories,* but I thwarted them. When the lights were turned down and the movie started, I was immediately transported into that beautiful realm of make-believe I loved so much and still do.

Fort Lewis, Washington

After our third zero week, the Army decided that this was a waste of time and manpower, even by their standards. They divided us up into groups and sent us to other camps throughout the Midwest and the far west. Our group of seventeen was assigned to the ASA, so they kept us intact. The other members of our battalion were sent to Army bases around the country. Our "adopted" son, Frankie, in fear and trembling, was sent to Fort Polk, Louisiana, which was famous for its rattlesnakes. We were sent to Fort Lewis, Washington. Bob and I waved goodbye to Frankie as his bus left for the train station. His face was pressed against the window, and his eyes were damp. I often wondered what happened to him. I hoped for the best, but feared the worst.

The Army can be difficult for guys like Frankie. The Army calls them misfits, and they're shown little sympathy or compassion, especially during Basic Training. They're usually smart, sometimes well educated, and always sensitive. The Army insists that soldiers all march to the same drummer, which is something these guys have never done in their lives. They find themselves being commanded to do things they find baffling and overwhelming. They're punished for not understanding the difference between the right way, the wrong way, and the "Army way."

The train ride to Fort Lewis was quite an adventure. It took us two days and one night, and we had one whole car on the train. We were three cars back from the dining car, which meant that we had to walk through three cars filled with civilians in order to eat. We were told that we couldn't look at the civilians, nor could we look out the windows while marching through their cars. We had to look straight ahead. This was my first indication that being a soldier in peacetime wasn't exactly the same as being a soldier during a war. Civilians knew we weren't keeping their country safe, and what they suspected was that we wanted to make the lives of their womenfolk very *unsafe*.

I'd only been in the Army about a month, when I recognized that I probably wasn't cut out to be a soldier, even though I wore a uniform and was bound to obey the Army's rules. My two guiding principles at that time in my life were: 1) Does this make sense? and 2) Is this fair?

I'd already concluded that much of what was being done to us violated both of those principles, and I didn't assume it was going to get much better.

Our train ride ended in Tacoma, Washington, which is the city nearest to Fort Lewis. The seventeen of us were ordered to board an Army bus that drove us to the fort. It was a beautiful, bright, sunny day. We could see snow-capped Mount Rainier. The trip lasted about twenty minutes. As I was getting off the bus, I heard a loud voice in a strong, southern accent yelling at somebody. I looked around and realized that I was the one being yelled at. I was wearing prescription sunglasses, and the man behind the voice grabbed my glasses off of my face. He then broke them in half and shattered each lens with the end of a stick he was carrying, that I later learned was aptly called a swagger stick.

He was yelling, "Trooper, there ain't but one got-damned soldier in this got-damned Army who can wear sunglasses. And you don't play no got-damned guitar."

Elvis had been drafted into the military about six months prior to our entering. I assumed that was who this rather angry and very loud sergeant was referring to. I was very upset, because he'd broken my prescription sunglasses, so I told him as politely as I could that my sunglasses were prescription, and I had a doctor's order to wear them. I told him my eyes became extremely bloodshot if I was in bright sunlight for long periods. The sergeant didn't seem to think that was a valid reason, and he reminded me again that I didn't play any got-damned guitar. I wasn't sure how he knew that, or what that had to do with my eye problem, but obviously the discussion was over.

After the sergeant was certain that no one else was wearing sunglasses, we were all assigned to companies. I was in Company A, and my company sergeant was Sergeant Eagle. Bob was in Company B, and his sergeant was the one who'd broken my sunglasses. His name was Sergeant Davis.

I never found out if Sgt. Eagle was part Native American, but Eagle seemed more like an apt description than a family name. He was medium height, thin, and wiry, with a large beaked nose, steely-gray eyes, and the cheekbones of a cadaver. He commanded respect, and we all responded accordingly.

He took all of Company A into a barracks that looked exactly like the wooden barracks at Fort Leonard Wood, and assigned us to bunks. There were twelve bunks on each side of the floor, and there were two floors in each barracks. At the end of the first floor, there was a latrine that contained eight showerheads, ten sinks, and ten toilets, all of which were in the open with about two feet of open space between them. The toilets were so close together that if a trooper were so inclined, and the trooper next to him was reading a magazine, they could both read it together. There were also other experiences you and every other person in that row shared, whether you wanted to or not. This new adventure in community living took some getting used to. Many of the guys learned to time their nature calls for when the latrine was almost empty.

The other end of the first floor was a private room for Sgt. Eagle. Each company had about fifty men, and there were three companies in our battalion. We were part of the 37th Infantry Battalion, and on our arm patch was the profile of an Indian head. The battalion motto was: "The Rock of the Marne." The battalion named it after a battle in World War I on the Marne River. We spent the rest of our first day sewing on our patches and learning how to store our equipment.

Our mornings started at five o'clock. We were given time to wash, get dressed, make our beds, and then report to the mess hall for breakfast.

The main reason I was skinny was that I was a very picky eater. When I first joined the Army, I was a little apprehensive when I learned that the mess halls didn't have a menu to choose from. Our choices were to eat what they had or go hungry. This was something my parents probably should have also done. I didn't gain weight in Basic Training, but I did learn to eat just about everything the Army served, except I drew the line at okra, no matter how they prepared it.

I soon found myself looking forward to breakfast, because I did like eggs and pancakes. I also learned to love SOS (shit on a shingle), which was chipped beef on toast. Lunches were complete, hot meals usually served with meat, vegetables, and dessert, which was normally ice cream, but sometimes cake or pie. Dinner was also a full meal, and depending on the mood of the cooks, was often very tasty. The Army bought the best food; the meat was always USDA Prime or better, and the vegetables were fresh. However, during my entire stay in the Army, I was always amazed that Army gravy tasted terrible, no matter where it was made or who made it. I believe that it was made from the grease in the pans, along with some flour. I knew from experience that the pans weren't always completely clean. Greasy water and soap do not lend themselves to tasty gravy.

The purpose of Basic Training was to turn civilians into soldiers. I understood that and tried to cooperate as best I could. Some people take to it like a duck to water. When asked a question by a sergeant, they respond loud and clear. When told to clean the latrine, it comes out spotless.

Below the shelves, we hung our uniforms in a particular order. The obedient soldiers' fatigues were pressed and cleaned, and their bunks were always ship-shape. Behind each bunk was a small clothes rack and a shelf. It was for our Dopp kits (toiletry bags named after early twentieth century leather craftsman, Charles Doppelt), in which we stored our soap and shaving materials. Those who were inclined to be good soldiers somehow knew how to do all the things that were demanded of them. I, on the other hand, didn't seem to be so inclined. I considered myself a normally fast and adroit learner, but I think my attitude got in the way of my being a good soldier.

Having cruised through high school, I thought I could do the same in the Army, at least through Basic Training. Sgt. Eagle didn't agree. It didn't take him long to learn where my bunk was. In fact, he didn't *need* to know where it was, because most of the time when he entered either door, he'd yell, "Teachman, give me twenty!"

The twenty he referred to wasn't currency, but rather push-ups.

I only weighed 133 pounds, so twenty push-ups weren't difficult to do, but after a few days, I became a little irritated at what I perceived to be the sergeant's biased behavior. The next time he entered and yelled, "Teachman, give me twenty!" I walked up to him and said:

"Excuse me, Sergeant, before I do that, I want to introduce you to the rest of the platoon."

The guys laughed, and before Sgt. Eagle yelled, "Make it forty!" I was sure that I detected a slight smile.

We ate all our meals in the battalion mess hall. There was only one entrance and one exit. About six feet before the entrance was a chin-up bar, and before a soldier could enter, he had to do three chin-ups. For most of us, that was easy, but we had a couple of really big guys who could have licked anyone of us in a fight, but they had a hell of a time doing three chin-ups. It was the first time I ever felt that being skinny was an advantage.

When I joined the Army, I expected to travel and grow up a bit faster, but I didn't realize that I'd meet people who were in so many ways quite different from me. I grew up on the West Side of Detroit and could divide people my age into three categories: hoodlums, college boys, and independents. I was basically a college boy with hoodlum friends. Even though I had seldom, if ever, traveled over to the East Side of Detroit, I assumed that people over there were just about like the people I knew.

In my company, there were good ol' boys from Georgia whom I could barely understand. They'd say something and I'd ask them to please repeat themselves. They would, and I still couldn't understand them. Instead of asking a third time, I would smile and say, "Oh."

There were guys from New York who didn't have driver's licenses, which I couldn't believe. For my friends and me, a driver's license was like killing your first lion. Getting a license meant you were a man and were one step closer to independence. *I* couldn't understand not wanting one, and *they* couldn't understand the need for one.

We had one guy who was from Italy. He joined the Army so that he could get his citizenship in three years instead of five. We got our first pay the second week of Basic Training. The Army pays in cash, and the men in each company lined up in alphabetical order in front of the paymaster, who's usually an officer. My Italian friend's name was Salvador Alessi, so he was first in line. The lieutenant looked for his name on the pay list, but couldn't find it.

He smiled at Private Alessi and said, "Your name isn't on the list, Private. There must be a mistake. You'll get paid when we get this straightened out."

"Thatsa all right, sir. No pay, no work," and he saluted the officer and walked away. I thought Sal's logic was irrefutable, but the Army didn't.

The second week of Basic Training, I went to the dispensary to get new prescription glasses, because my eyes were constantly bloodshot. While I sat there with about five other soldiers who were also waiting, a doctor came out and asked if any of us were *not* sick. I hesitated a moment, because that sounded like a trick question, but the doctor looked serious, so I raised my hand. He told me to leave immediately. I was going to protest, but his voice carried a sense of urgency that made me follow his orders quickly. Two days later, most of my company and I had the Asian flu.

Most soldiers who returned from duty in Japan and Korea came in through Fort Lewis before they were shipped elsewhere. The Asian flu came there first, then swept across the country. Most of us were confined to our barracks and bed for about three or four days before we all resumed our Basic Training cycle.

One day after we finished being instructed in marching in formation, our company was marched out to the practice field. We were told to get into a straight line from one side of the field to the other and start marching. After a moment, we were given the order to run. Then the sergeant yelled:

"Hit the dirt!"

We all flung ourselves to the ground. My right knee landed on a sharp rock that tore through my fatigues and cut a gash in my knee. The sergeant told us to get up, march, run, and then again yelled, "Hit the dirt!"

I stopped, sat down, then laid down.

Sgt. Eagle ran up to me yelling, "Teachman, if this were war, you'd be dead."

I said, "Sergeant, if this were war, I'd hit the dirt, but this isn't war, and I've already messed up one pair of fatigues and one knee."

After I gave him my twenty push-ups, he let me get my knee examined.

Another day while I was on KP again, a young man with glasses and a very frightened look was trying to obey the mess sergeant's order to clean the oven racks. The ovens had just been used, so the racks were very hot. The young man tried to pull out one of the racks and burned his fingers. I watched him do it, and before he tried to do it again, I went over to him and handed him the hook that was hanging from the side of the oven. I showed him how to use it to pull the rack out and told him to dip the rack into the cold water in the sink. He gave me the same look that Frankie had given me back at Fort Leonard Wood when I untangled him from his shirt. This guy's name was Henry, he was from Chicago, and he was a genius.

Henry graduated from the University of Chicago at fifteen years old, finished law school at eighteen, and became a CPA by the time he was twenty. He knew he was going to be drafted, so he applied for an officer's commission. However, he was drafted before his commission came through. The Army decided he had to go through Basic Training before he'd be commissioned as a first lieutenant and sent to the Adjutant General Corps.

I soon realized that I had another adopted son who looked to me for a certain amount of guidance. Henry, like everyone else in my company, knew that I was never going to be soldier of the month, but I wasn't picked on like Henry was. That was somewhat of a puzzle to me. I think the main difference between us— other than the fact that Henry was a genius and Frankie may have been one, too—was that my resistance was a choice. Theirs was not an unwillingness to play the game, but rather a complete lack of knowledge of how the game was played.

Another problem for Henry was that the sergeants knew that he was going to be a first lieutenant. Most of the sergeants believed that Henry was a misfit and didn't belong in their Army; Henry received more than his fair share of orders to hit the deck and give whatever non-commissioned officer (NCO) was there, twenty or thirty push-ups. Since Henry was heavier than I was and not athletic, the push-ups were a little difficult for him, but he never failed to attempt to obey the orders.

I gave Henry a great deal of credit for putting up with the mental abuse that was heaped upon him, and I hoped our friendship helped him handle some of that. When graduation day came, the captain told Henry that at the end of the ceremony, he'd be called forward to receive his first lieutenant's bars. The captain said that Henry's first salute would go to him, as his commanding officer, and he could then designate someone, such as a family member, to receive his second salute. Since his family was in Chicago and they weren't attending the ceremony, Henry asked if I could be that designated person. I don't think that thrilled the captain, but he allowed it.

After Henry received the bars on his shoulders by the captain, he raised his right hand and saluted the captain smartly. I was standing to the right of the captain. Henry turned slightly, smiled at me, and saluted me—with his left hand. I kept a straight face, but I could feel the captain's rage.

☆ ☆ ☆

There was one guy from California who claimed he was on the verge of stardom when he was drafted. Naturally, we all called him Hollywood. Most of the guys didn't believe him, even though he was much better-looking than most of us. He told me one day during chow that he had the same agent as Tab Hunter.

I said, "I went to high school with a guy who has that agent. His real name is Jim Westmoreland, but his stage name is Rod Fulton."

Hollywood said, "You're kidding. I know Rod. He's a big guy, about 6'3" and almost 200 pounds, with black, curly hair."

That description fit the guy I knew, and I started to believe Hollywood. We became friendly.

One day he said, "I'm not going to let the Army fuck up my chances for fame and fortune."

After a hard day of climbing ropes and wooden barriers, Hollywood went to the dispensary, complaining of back pain. At first, the Army didn't believe him. Back injuries in those days were hard to prove or disprove, and claiming a back injury was a favorite ploy of malingerers.

From that day on, Hollywood walked around stiffly with his right hand shoved down his belt and pressed against his back. Sergeants would walk up silently and yell at him. He never jumped. He would turn around slowly with a pained look on his face, and after looking at the sergeant with an expression of great sadness, turn around and limp away. It was an Academy Award–winning performance. After two weeks, he was sent to a hospital and didn't return. I never saw him in a movie and don't know if he got a medical discharge, but I do know that he was a talented actor.

☆ ☆ ☆

After six weeks, we were granted a twelve-hour pass on a Sunday. I took a bus to Tacoma and walked down the main street, feeling almost like a free man; I wore my full Army uniform: a freshly pressed khaki shirt and pants, Army tie and belt, spit-polished Army shoes, and my garrison cap. A middle-aged lady walked toward me, accompanied by a nice-looking younger woman who could have been her daughter. As they got closer, I smiled at both of them and said, "Good morning."

The older woman scowled as she stepped in front of the younger one, prepared to ward off my evil spirit, then she spit on the sidewalk in the area of my government-issued, spit-polished shoes. I kept walking, thinking that she assumed I was a soldier just because I was in uniform. She had no idea how wrong she was.

I saw a department store across the street and rushed in. I bought a civilian shirt and belt, and put my Army shirt, tie, cap, and belt in a shopping bag, and walked out of the store, a temporary civilian. I spent the rest of the day walking the streets of Tacoma saying hello to everyone I encountered. They couldn't have been nicer.

I found out that Tacoma wasn't unusual. There's a poem by Rudyard Kipling called "Tommy Atkins," which is the British equivalent of G.I. Joe. Kipling describes how the general population mistreats soldiers in peacetime, then politely calls on them to protect them during war. I was angry at that lady who spat at my boots. I felt unfairly treated. However, after being in the Army a few months and watching how so many GIs misbehaved in public while on leave, I had a better understanding of her actions.

Soldiers are mostly young boys away from home for the first time, and some of them don't handle that newfound freedom very well. When they get drunk, they act like fools. Drunken soldiers fall into four categories:

- they get maudlin and cry a lot;

- they get sloppy and spill beer over themselves and whoever's near them;

- they pick fights; and

- a small number have a good time.

I came to realize that it was prudent for people in Army towns to stay clear of all soldiers who drank. But I also wished that people would be nice to the well-behaved soldiers after they got to know them.

About the third week of Basic Training, Sgt. Eagle introduced us to the M1 rifle. I'd fired a gun once when I was twelve. I'd killed a bird on my grandma's farm with a BB gun and buried the bird with tears in my eyes. Whenever my father had too much to drink, he'd ask me if I wanted to go hunting and fishing with him someday in the Rockies. I always said yes, knowing that day would never come, and also knowing that I had absolutely no desire to hunt or fish, and neither did my dad. When Sgt. Eagle asked if any of us had ever fired a gun before, I was the only one who didn't raise his hand, which probably didn't surprise him.

The M1 is a semi-automatic rifle, which means that in order to load it, the bolt has to come back, which drops a shell into the chamber and then slams shut. Sgt. Eagle's main lesson was showing us how to do that without getting our thumb smashed by the bolt, which is called an M1 thumb, and it hurts like hell. After he demonstrated how to do it safely and correctly, he asked me to try it. If any of my fellow soldiers had been given a chance, they would have given big odds that I would end up with an M1 thumb, and they would've been correct. Sgt. Eagle just smiled.

My next encounter with the M1 was on the 1,000-inch range, a short rifle range where soldiers are instructed by an NCO on how to fire the M1. The soldiers lie prone, and the sergeants kneel next to them. The first shot I fired ejected a hot shell that went right down my back, inside my fatigue shirt, and burned my skin.

I looked at the sergeant and said, "You'd better take this thing before I kill myself or somebody else."

He understood and encouraged me to give it another try. The rest of the session went better. I learned how to shoot and not injure anyone, including myself.

When it came time to qualify with the M1, we all went down

to the range. Each soldier had to fire a certain number of rounds at targets that were 200, 300, and 500 yards away. Each soldier had to do that from four different positions: standing, sitting, kneeling, and prone. I did all right from the standing position with the target being 200 yards away, and I did less well from the sitting and kneeling positions, where the targets were 300 yards away. I surprised myself, and my sergeants, by getting eight out of ten bulls' eyes from the prone position, where the target was 500 yards away.

I gained new respect for the Army's teaching ability. I begrudgingly admitted that they took someone with no experience and a strong bias against ever learning, and taught him how to shoot a rifle with a fair degree of accuracy.

The Army spent a great deal of time and energy convincing each of us that our lives depended on our rifles, and they were never to be called guns. We learned how to take them apart very quickly and put them back together blindfolded. I actually became very proficient at both tasks, which delighted Sgt. Eagle. Keeping the rifle clean and well-oiled was our top priority.

One day after we'd all qualified with our rifles, we went to a shooting range near the edge of the woods. It had pop-up targets of various colors. The sergeant would have a different-colored target pop up and would ask one of us to estimate how far we were from each target. I knew this was going to be problematic for me, because of my color blindness.

I was tested for color blindness while working at Ford Motor Company in 1957; I was diagnosed as fairly severe. They showed me twenty circles on a screen, one at a time. Each circle had lots of different-colored dots, some of which formed a number that anyone who isn't colorblind could see. I saw one number out of twenty.

When my turn came, the sergeant popped a target and asked me how far away it was. I looked at the woods and then at the sergeant and asked, "What target, Sergeant?"

He said, "The red one."

"I don't see a red target, Sergeant."

"What the hell are you? Blind?" he screamed, even though I was right next to him, which I was never able to get used to.

"No, Sergeant, and I'm not deaf either, but I am colorblind."

For the next ten minutes, he called over all of the NCOs and a few officers. He would pop up a target and ask me to estimate how far away it was.

I asked, "What target, Sergeant?"

He laughed and told his friends, "Can you believe it? This poor excuse for a soldier is fucking colorblind."

Then they all laughed together.

We would periodically have rifle inspections.

At one rifle inspection, after the target range episode, the lieutenant gripped my rifle and inspected it by looking down the barrel. I had intentionally placed a few drops of water down the barrel two days before.

After looking down the barrel of my rifle, he yelled at me, "What the hell, trooper, your rifle is filled with rust. Can't you see that?"

Sgt. Eagle looked at him and said, "He's colorblind, sir. He can't see rust." Sgt Eagle instructed the trooper whose bunk was next to mine to make sure my rifle was rust-free for the next inspection. The trooper said he would, but knew it wouldn't be necessary.

☆ ☆ ☆

We were also taught how to stand guard duty, which, according to the Army, involves quite a bit more than just standing. If someone approached us, we were to say, "Halt. Who goes there?"

When the person responded, we were then to say, "Advance and be recognized."

When the person got within fifteen feet of us, we were to then say, "Halt," and determine who it was.

The first night I was on guard duty, I was guarding a building that was surrounded by a fence. I had to walk around the building to make sure no one entered. At one point, I saw an officer approaching on the other side of the fence.

"Halt. Who goes there?" I commanded.

"Lieutenant Moore," he answered.

He was about thirty feet from me, but about fifteen feet from the fence that separated us. I said to him, "Advance and be recognized."

He stepped toward me and walked right into the fence. I was shocked and hoped he wasn't hurt.

He yelled at me, "Trooper, you're supposed to tell me to halt."

I looked at him and said, "Sir, I didn't think that was necessary."

"Your job is not to fucking think, trooper. You're to follow fucking procedures, which includes telling the person to halt."

"Even if I know the person *has* to halt, sir?" I asked.

"You have to follow all the rules, trooper, every time you're on guard duty. If you don't, your ass will be mine."

Sgt. Eagle turned out to be a really good guy. We all developed a great deal of respect for him, both as a man and a sergeant. Our platoon even bought him a watch that we presented to him on the last evening of our training cycle.

Sgt. Davis, who was Bob's platoon sergeant, was more problematic. He was probably a nice guy and never showed any meanness, even toward Henry, but he lacked school smarts or street smarts, or more likely, both. The movie, *DI*, which starred Jack Webb playing a tough Marine drill instructor, was released that spring, and we were all sure that Sgt. Davis had seen it at least four times. He tried to become Jack Webb's character, but he wasn't able to make himself believable. He knew how to strut, and he memorized all of Webb's lines, but there was always something missing, and he ended up looking more like Gomer Pyle than Jack Webb.

There was a master sergeant in the battalion who was rumored to have been an airborne ranger in Korea. He was about thirty-five years old, Black, and built like a fullback. Every once in a while, we'd see him practicing throwing a bayonet; he never missed. Sgt. Davis also watched him.

One day, Sgt. Davis figured he would teach us about the bayonet. He called us into formation and proceeded to instruct us on the use of this lethal tool that he awkwardly switched from hand to hand, as if it were too hot to handle. He looked menacing and shouted:

"This here is a bayonet. In the right hands, this here bayonet is a lethal weapon. Do you all understand what I'm saying?"

We responded, "Yes, Sergeant."

Anytime a sergeant asked a soldier of lesser rank a question, the response had to end with "Sergeant," stated loud and clear.

"I did not hear you!" he bellowed.

"Yes, Sergeant!" we yelled back.

"I still did not hear you!" he yelled in his best Jack Webb accent.

"Yes, Sergeant!" we answered a little louder than the previous time. He wasn't happy, but he continued, "This here weapon has one purpose, and that is to kill. The spirit of the bayonet is to kill. Do you troopers understand that?"

"Yes, Sergeant," came our weak reply.

He let it pass, because he was ready with his next question: "What is the spirit of the bayonet?"

In our loudest reply of the day, as if we'd rehearsed it, we trumpeted, "To kill sergeants."

Sgt. Davis looked at us for a minute, wondering if he'd heard correctly, and then dismissed us.

I only had one more conversation with Sgt. Davis, and that was on the last day of bivouac (the Army's version of camping out), while taking a smoke break. I didn't smoke before I enlisted, but the first week in Basic Training, the sergeant gave us a break and said, "Take ten. Smoke if you got 'em."

And then he said, "Teachman, police the area."

I said, "Why me, Sergeant?"

"Because you don't smoke."

That evening, after mess hall, I bought my first, but not my last, carton of cigarettes.

During the break, Sgt. Davis said to me, "This has been a tough cycle for me. I'll be glad when it's over and I can go back home to the West Coast."

"Aren't you from North Carolina, Sergeant?" I asked.

He said, "Yeh."

"That's the East Coast, Sergeant," I replied.

He looked at me apologetically and said, "I always get those two mixed up."

We got our next twenty-four-hour pass the weekend after we finished our sixth week of Basic Training. After breakfast on the following Monday morning, I was walking back to the barracks and enjoying the view of snow-capped Mt. Rainier, when I felt a strange sensation in my throat. I had my first bout of strep throat when I was about twelve years old and my second bout around sixteen. I learned from the second experience that if I got a shot of penicillin right away, it shortened the pain and duration of the infection considerably.

I immediately went to the dispensary and placed myself on sick call. A nurse called my name, and I went into an exam room. The Army believes that the surest way to separate the sick from the malingerers is to take their temperatures. Before I could explain to her that my average temperature was about 97.6 degrees, she stuck a thermometer in my mouth. When she took it out, a doctor entered the room and looked at the reading.

"Your temp is 99.1. You're not sick," the doctor remarked.

"Sir, my average temperature is 97.6," I explained.

"Bullshit. You had a twenty-four-hour pass. Got mixed up with some floozy and didn't want to protect yourself," he declared with a certain smugness.

"No, sir, I've had strep throat twice before, and I know the symptoms," I explained.

"So now you're a doctor? Get your lying ass out of here, trooper, before I call the MPs," he threatened.

I was back to the dispensary the next morning with a temperature of 101.4 degrees. There was a different doctor on duty, and after looking at my throat, he said I had a serious case of strep throat. I had to hold my tongue.

"Your company is going on a fifteen-mile hike tomorrow, aren't you?" he asked me.

"Yes, sir," I replied.

"You can't miss that; they might recycle you [meaning I'd have to start Basic Training all over again]. I'll give you a shot that will straighten you out, so that you'll be able to make that hike," he said.

"Thank you, sir," I said politely.

He gave me a shot in my right hip, and my strep throat was gone by nightfall.

The next morning, I got out of bed and almost fell over. I could hardly move my right hip, and when I tried, it hurt like hell. I limped over to the mess hall. I hoped by moving it a bit, the pain would lessen. Then I took a couple of aspirins and hoped for the best. No matter what I did, I could not walk without favoring my right hip.

At the gathering area for the hike, we formed into columns about 8:00 a.m. The lieutenant led the platoon for our fifteen-mile hike and counted cadence: "Hep, two, three, four," which everybody followed but me. I was marching to my own drumbeat: "Hep, ouch, two ouch, four ouch."

Sgt. Eagle ran up to me and yelled, "What the fuck are you doing? Waltzing?"

"No, Sergeant, I got a shot in my hip yesterday, and it hurts," I answered.

"You got a shot? With a tiny little needle? And it hurts," he said mockingly.

"I didn't see the size of the needle, Sergeant, but yes, it hurts like hell," I said.

"Well, it will hurt a fuck of a lot worse if you don't shape up. You're making my platoon look stupid," he said.

At this point, the whole platoon started limping to my cadence. I figured this was going to drive Sgt. Eagle nuts, but he just kept marching alongside us. I swore he was smiling. I think he liked the fact that the whole platoon stood up for me. They marched to my drumbeat for about five minutes and then went back to the normal cadence. By this time, the aspirins had started to kick in, and I was almost able to keep up. After a mile or so, my hip was either numb or the pain was gone. The rest of the hike went smoothly. Apparently, the lieutenant hadn't noticed a thing.

I found out after my discharge about three years later that the antibiotic I'd been given not only killed strep bacteria, but also every healthy bacterium in the intestinal tract. It took me years to restore its balance.

☆ ☆ ☆

The platoon developed an unwritten code that we all followed, which was based on trust. When we went to shower, we'd empty our pockets, take off our watches, and lay it all on our beds, knowing that nobody would touch a thing. That trust carried over to our card playing. After every payday, there were a number of fairly high-stakes games. The better players usually won, and the bad players usually lost, but every once in a while, somebody would get very lucky.

One of the guys from Chicago seemed to be lucky more than his share of the time. Eventually, they caught him cheating and gave him a GI shower: that is, they took him into the shower, stripped him down to his skivvies, and scrubbed him raw with scrub brushes. He was laid up for a couple of days, and Sgt. Eagle looked the other way. This guy had been an all-around troublemaker and a bully, but after his "shower," he pretty much straightened out and kept to himself. I'd like to think he learned his lesson.

In Detroit, my friends and I did a lot of teasing as we hung out on the corner or in the poolroom. We called it "pimping," and I soon learned that guys from the New York area called it "busting balls." I received more than my share from my platoon mates, but I was able to give it back when some went too far. I was surprised and pleased when I realized that no one in our platoon picked on the truly vulnerable.

There was one guy named Emerson who was about 5'5" tall and sounded very effeminate. He was always in a good mood and could be quite entertaining. He had a prominent scar on his cheek, and when asked how he got it, his stock answer was, "An elephant bit me." A lot of the guys assumed he was gay, and commented on the fact that he was the first one in the shower and the last one out, but no one teased him or bullied him. In fact, he was generally well accepted by all of us. I was fairly sure that Emerson wouldn't have stood a chance in my poolroom, which gave me my first inkling that an "Army buddy" might be a different breed of friendship.

The last week of Basic Training included bivouac. The whole battalion marched out into the woods, which made up most of the area that is Fort Lewis. We pitched tents, played war games, and stood guard duty. I had never camped and wasn't that fond of being in the woods, especially around dusk and at night. My few visits to the woods in Michigan consisted primarily of me trying to hide unsuccessfully from huge Michigan mosquitoes.

I was pleased to discover that the woods in Washington State were different. There were no mosquitoes, but there were thousands of bees. Joe, one of our guys from New Jersey, was allergic to bee stings and was extremely nervous around them. The bees buzzed around us like flies, but they never landed on us. The only danger of getting stung was if you sat on one. Joe tried to stay standing as long as he could and managed to survive the week without one bite. We were all happy when bivouac was over, but Joe was ecstatic—and very tired.

The last night of bivouac, I was scheduled to stand guard duty from midnight until 4:00 a.m. The sergeant took me into the woods to the perimeter of our area, and I relieved the guy who was on duty. The sergeant told me that someone would be back at 4:00 to relieve me. I didn't like being out there alone in the dark, and it was *very* dark. I started to hear things and see things that I knew were not mosquitoes, and I also knew they were out to do me no good.

I must have fallen asleep, because when I woke up, I didn't know what time it was, but I was sure it was past 4:00 a.m. I figured they'd forgotten about me. I ran to what I thought was our area. I was sure there was somebody or something running behind me. I changed directions, and after what felt like days, emerged into an area of tents with a sigh of relief.

After looking around, I realized that it didn't look like my platoon. I desperately searched for Sgt. Eagle's tent, which was larger, because he shared it with another sergeant. When I finally found it, I was able to locate my tent. After I got into my cot, I worried for a moment that my relief was out there looking for me, but I knew there was no way I was going back out into those woods. I lay there wide awake until morning and wondered what they were going to do to me. Falling asleep on guard duty is the Army's equivalent of a mortal sin.

We all went to the mess tent, and no one was looking for me, but a little after 8:00 p.m., a friend of mine came up to me and asked, "Where in the hell were you? I came to relieve you and called out your name a few times. When you didn't answer, I figured you were asleep and would wake up with the sun."

I explained what happened, and he walked away laughing. That was the first and last time in my life that I went camping.

Basic Training ended with all the recruits crawling along on their stomachs under strings of barbed wire over an area about the size of a football field. There were ten lanes, and you had to stay in your lane. There was a machine gun at the far end of the field that steadily fired live ammunition about five or six feet above the field, ensuring that the recruits crawled on their stomachs the whole distance. The machine gun's field of fire was about two lanes wide, which meant the gun had to swing from one side of the field to the other in a regular pattern. Since it was nighttime and dark, a few guys timed the intervals and would get up and run when the gunfire wasn't covering their lanes. I decided not to try that. I covered the entire distance on my stomach as close as I could get to the ground.

We were all dressed for night combat, with black shoe polish on our faces and hands. When our platoon finished, we all went back to the barracks, cleaned up, and celebrated. A group of guys decided to give Sgt. Eagle a gift. We all chipped in and bought him a watch. We presented it to him that night. The next day, which was a Saturday, we were part of a graduation ceremony on the Fort Lewis parade grounds, after which we received our travel orders and travel pay.

☆ ☆ ☆

Our final month's pay was about $72. My travel pay to my next duty station, which was Fort Devens in Massachusetts, was about $150. That was more money than any of us had had in our pockets in quite a while.

Naturally, most of us played poker. We were playing, and I was getting good cards. I was up about $140 when we called last hand. It was seven-card stud. I was dealt a pair of queens in the hole and an ace faceup. I bet $2, and everyone stayed. My second up card was another ace. I raised the bet to $4, and three guys stayed. One guy had two up cards to a straight, and another guy, two up cards to a flush. The third guy was losing big, because he stayed in almost every hand. He had a ten and a three showing. I bet $4, and the flush guy raised the bet to $8. Everyone called, including the guy with the ten and the three, which was no surprise to any of us.

The next card I received was a six and no help. The guy with the possible straight got no help, and neither did the nothing hand. The guy with two hearts got another heart. I checked, and he bet $4, which was the limit until the last card. We all stayed. The last up for me was a queen, which gave me a full house. The straight got help, the flush didn't, and the third guy got a three, which gave him a pair of threes, showing. I bet $4, was raised $4 by the flush, and the straight raised a third $4. The pair of threes stayed.

One guy who wasn't in the hand said to the guy with the threes, "You're facing a straight, a flush, and probably a full house. Why in the hell are you staying?"

He just muttered, "I know, I know."

After the last card, I bet the maximum: $8. The flush stayed and the straight dropped. I figured I was golden. The guy with a pair of threes would have to have four threes, and he would have to get two of them on his last two cards. The odds were overwhelmingly in my favor, and he couldn't have four threes, because he'd just called my bet. But I was wrong. He did have four threes. We were all stunned. He was a good guy, just a bad poker player. He just about broke even, which was good for him, and I lost about $40 of my winnings.

We were granted two weeks' leave and two weeks for travel time after Basic Training. The last three days of Basic Training, I experienced an attack of acute gastritis for the first time in my life. I didn't go to the dispensary at the time, because I didn't know it was gastritis. All I knew was that it came and went and was extremely painful. I didn't go to the doctors, because the Army has a habit of recycling people who are ill. With the help of my friends, I struggled through those last three days.

When the bus left Fort Lewis for the airport in Tacoma, Washington, I'd already started to feel better. By the time we got to the airport, my stomach was totally calm, and I was hungry, because I hadn't eaten in three days. That was also the first time I realized that my brain had a lot to do with the way I felt. Whatever disease I had, I felt it was probably caused by anxiety and was cured when the anxiety left me.

When I arrived home, my mother said I looked pale and sickly. I weighed even less than I had when I went into the Army. But in two to three days, I felt normal again, and my color was back. Plus, I gained a couple of pounds.

☆ ☆ ☆

The Army allows you two weeks of travel time to get to your next duty, because soldiers used to travel most often by train. By flying home and flying to my next duty, I was home almost twenty-eight days. My father complained to my mother that I was home more since joining the Army than when I was living at home.

The most interesting thing I experienced while at home was the realization that none of my friends missed me while I was gone. Most of them didn't even realize I'd been gone for three months. At nineteen years old, I believed that when I left a place like home, that part of the world stopped and waited to resume only when I got back. I found out that wasn't true.

CHAPTER 2

My Time at Fort Devens

After my leave was up, I flew to Fort Devens, Massachusetts, which was the home of the ASA Training Center and School. It was also the place where ASA recruits, fresh out of Basic Training, were tested and assigned to different schools.

When we arrived at Fort Devens, they assigned us to barracks and bunks. For the first three days following the Army rule of no sitting around, they assigned us to KP, policing the areas and whatever jobs the sergeants felt would keep us busy. Bob and I resumed honing our new skill of bugging out—that is, doing as little Army "busy work" as possible. We would show up for muster (accounting for members in a military unit) in the mornings after breakfast, along with all the other soldiers who were waiting to be tested.

There were probably sixty soldiers, including the seventeen from Michigan, who went through Basic Training with us. All seventeen of us wanted to go to the Army Language School, which was in Monterey, California, and provided college credits after you got out of the Army. Bob and I were assured by our recruiting sergeant that we would be assigned to the Language School. We naively believed him.

The two oldest soldiers in our company, who'd been in the service before, knew better. They said we would all be tested to determine who would go to the Language School. That was somewhat of a shock, but Bob and I were both fairly good test takers and were confident that we'd pass.

The morning we were to take the test, the lieutenant divided the sixty soldiers into three groups of twenty each, and then our sergeant started marching us over to the test center. Fort Devens is a very large fort, about 5,000 acres, and apparently has a complicated layout. Our sergeant got us lost. We marched around much of the area until we found the test center. Unfortunately, we arrived after the Language School test had been administered.

The sergeants at the testing area took the twenty of us and assigned us to Code School, which made no one happy. We heard rumors from other ASA people that Code School had the highest rate of alcoholism of any of the ASA schools. Apparently, all they did for eight hours a day was listen to dot, dot, and dash.

I believed the rumors, and I was also extremely upset that I was denied the chance to take the test. I called my parents when we got back to our barracks and told them the bad news. I could tell that my father had been drinking, and he could tell I was upset. He told me that he'd take me hunting and fishing in the Rockies when I came home for Christmas. I smiled to myself and said, "Okay, Dad."

We were all sitting around complaining, when someone uttered the classic Army response: "Tell it to the chaplain."

I said, "That's a great idea."

I got up, started down to the chapel at the end of our lane, and walked into the chaplain's office. None of the other guys, including Bob, came with me; in fact, most of them laughed at me. The chaplain politely listened to my tale of woe, and after hearing the whole story, agreed that it wasn't fair that I didn't get a chance to compete for something that had been promised to me by my lying recruiter.

He called the testing area and asked when the next test would be given for the Language School. He was told they were forming a new group, and the first test would be in two days. He told them he was going to send a soldier named Private Gerard Teachman over there to be tested.

I asked the chaplain if he'd also include Pvt. Robert McCall, and he did. Then he went one step further, which had a huge effect on the rest of my life. He asked the soldier in the testing area what score was needed in order to qualify. He was told that a perfect score was fifty-two. Why fifty-two? Only the Army knew. The soldier felt a forty or better would be sufficient. He also told the chaplain that the Army had a different way of scoring than most other institutions. The Army gave one point for a correct answer and subtracted two points for a wrong answer. He told the chaplain to advise me not to guess, and to only write down answers that I was relatively sure were correct. I thanked the chaplain profusely and went back to the barracks. My friends, including Bob, were still sitting there. One of them asked me, "Did the chaplain laugh at you?"

I said no, and proceeded to tell them that Bob and I were getting a chance to take the test in two days.

They all moaned a bit, and then one asked, "Why didn't you give them all of our names?"

I reminded him that the chaplain's office was just down at the end of the street. Not one of them made that trip.

Bob and I took the test two days later, along with about eighty other soldiers. The test was a form of Esperanto and was about thirty-five minutes long. A grammatical rule would be explained in a paragraph, and then there would be two or three questions, either multiple choice or true and false on each paragraph. I finished forty questions and still had time to spare, so I reviewed each of the forty answers to make sure that each one was correct. Then I did six more questions, and I was also confident that these answers were correct. The time was up. The tests were corrected on the spot. They told us they were taking the top three. I had the top score for that day, which was forty-six. Someone else was second, and Bob was third.

As the top three, we were told to list the three languages that we wanted, in order of preference. Bob and I wanted most of all to go to Europe, and German was the best bet, so we both picked that language as our first choice, and Serbo-Croatian as our second language, our thinking being that Serbo-Croatian is spoken in what was then Yugoslavia. We couldn't be sent to Yugoslavia, but we would probably be sent to Germany. Our third choice was Russian, because we knew that Russian was the largest class at the Language School. Most Russian students were sent to Germany, but they were also sent to Japan, Alaska, and Turkey.

I was assigned German, and Bob was assigned Russian. We were told that I got German because I had the top score, and Bob got Russian because he had the third-highest score. If we'd known that was how they did it, Bob would've picked German as his third choice, and we both would have been assigned German. But in any case, Bob and I were thrilled that we were able to get assigned to the Army Language School.

It was ironic and kind of sad that in that group of eighty, there was a former colonel who'd once been the commanding officer of the Army Language School. Since the Army was downsizing, this colonel lost his officer's rank and was now a master sergeant. He had three years to go before he had his thirty years of service. He wanted to go back to the Language School as a student. He spoke to the group of eighty before the test and told us what a beautiful place the Language School was, and what an amazing duty it was. Unfortunately, he didn't make the cut. We heard that his final score was twelve.

The sergeant who got us lost did Bob and me such an enormous favor that we were always going to be in his debt. If we'd taken the test the day we were supposed to and had scored the same, I would have been number two. Number one scored a forty-eight, but that day, they only needed one more student to fill their quota, and he was assigned Chinese. The Language School course for Chinese was eighteen months long. And nobody who graduated from the Chinese course ever went anywhere near Europe.

A year later, I ran into the sergeant who got us lost. I was in a PX (a Post Exchange store—basically a department store for military personnel), in Nürnberg. I walked up to him and said, "You don't know me, but you did me the hugest favor I've ever received."

I told him my story and asked if I could buy him a drink. We shared a couple of beers.

He was stationed outside of Nürnberg in a town called Herzogenaurach (Herzo), which is an ASA station in southern Germany. I was in Herzo for three days, but was stationed in Coburg, which was another town about sixty miles north. I never saw the sergeant again, but I still remain grateful.

☆ ☆ ☆

We arrived in Fort Devens around the first of September. The new class that Bob and I were going to start at the Language School didn't begin until the first week of January. We had to stay at Fort Devens until the middle of December, then we could go home for

Christmas, and then on to California. Since we were going to be there for almost three months, Bob took a three-day pass, went home to Michigan, and drove his car back.

Those of us who were waiting for our new assignments were assigned to special barracks in order to satisfy the Army's "no standing around" rule. This means we were assigned to the "slave market." Each morning, bright and early, the sergeants would come to the market and pick out how many men they wanted. Each of us were assigned duties for the day: landscaping, policing the area (picking up cigarette butts), and KP. Bob and I viewed this as a direct challenge, because of our strong philosophical opposition to busy work, especially KP.

I met a soldier whose last name was Sanders. He was leaving to go to Monterey in the next shipment, which was the following week. He and I shared the same philosophy about the Army, so he gave me one of his name tags, which said "Sanders." I sewed it on one of my field jackets and showed up for the morning roster as Sanders. Each sergeant would pick his men, take their names, and assign them their daily duty. I would then stop in the barracks and switch fatigue jackets. Then I'd head for the one place I knew the sergeants would never look for me: the library. I don't remember what Bob's ruse was, but he also managed to get away, and we would meet at the library.

The sergeants had a funny sense of how the game was played. If they suspected something, they'd search rather diligently until they either found you and punished you, or until they didn't find you. They'd stop the search when they went to lunch. Afterward, they didn't seem to care. Bob and I were a little confused by this daily duty rule, until we found out that many of the duties to which the other guys were assigned ended at lunch, except for KP. Once we knew that, we realized that we were only in danger from about 7:00 in the morning until 1:00 in the afternoon.

We knew that the chances of our sergeants going to the library were even slimmer than going to church, but if we went to the library every day, the sergeants on duty in the library would get suspicious. At times, if the weather was nice, we hid in the woods. One time, the weather turned on us and we were cold. There was a car parked near the woods, so to get out of the heavy wind, we hid under the car. I looked at Bob and asked:

"Is it absolutely necessary that we never do any work for the Army? I think that it might be more comfortable doing something inside until noon, rather than lying out here on the cold ground freezing to death."

He looked at me and said, "It's become a matter of principle."

On another day, the sergeant came into our barracks and said he needed four volunteers. Normally, Bob and I never responded to such requests, but the weather was getting even colder. The sergeant continued by saying he needed four new firemen. We were both familiar with that duty and immediately volunteered.

Each of our barracks was heated by a huge coal furnace that was located in the furnace room at the end of the structure. Soldiers maintained the fire in these furnaces on a schedule of twenty-four hours on and twenty-four hours off, and then twenty-four hours on again and twenty-four off, and then twenty-four on and three days off. Bob and I realized that this schedule would allow us to go on some of the side trips that we wanted to take. Most of the time, the soldiers, waiting for transport to Monterey, would get at most a twenty-four-hour pass, or maybe thirty-six hours, but never longer.

A three-day pass would allow us to go to Boston and spend some time there, or go to our dream destination: New York City.

Bob and I were accepted as two of the new firemen. They sent us to fireman school for two days, and then each of us was assigned a barracks that we had to maintain. One of the new firemen was a guy from Southern California named John, and it was fun to watch him at the school. He knew what coal was, but never actually saw any. He'd never heard of clinkers (noncombustible elements found in coal that melt and fuse together as lumpy ashes from coal combustion), which are the nemeses of any coal furnace. We were warned that if a clinker formed while we were on duty, we would be severely punished.

Being from Michigan and growing up in homes with coal-burning furnaces, Bob and I were quite familiar with coal and clinkers. We became friends with John, gave him tips, and helped him out when necessary.

The difficult time for firemen was from 10:00 at night until 6:00 in the morning, because we had to tend to the fires and stay awake. These were the times when Bob, John, and I got together; helped one another; and talked. John was a jazz enthusiast, and Bob and I knew next to nothing about jazz, so John introduced us to his favorite musicians. He had records and a small record player, so we listened to jazz, and he taught us what he knew.

On our first three-day pass, Bob, two other guys, and I drove to New York City in Bob's car. We needed the two other guys to help pay for gas. Once in the city, they went their separate ways, and we agreed to meet at an agreed-upon time to drive back to Fort Devens. Bob and I checked into a hotel room near Times Square and went to a bar. You could drink in New York City at that time at eighteen years old, and for the first time in our lives, we drank in a bar legally. Over our drink, Bob proceeded to give me my instructions. He said our mission was to find two attractive women who wanted to be with us, something Bob knew wasn't going to be that difficult for *him*, but might be problematic for me. He said that the most important thing I had to remember was that no one was supposed to be able to recognize that we were in New York for the first time in our lives. Bob was sure that no attractive women were interested in tourists.

We set out to find these two women, and within a very short time, we were talking to two nice-looking girls from Vermont. They were obviously tourists. I wanted to point out the irony of this to Bob, but I decided not to. We took the girls to a couple of bars where jazz was playing, and we impressed them with the jazz knowledge we'd recently acquired from John. We all had a grand time, and the girl who was with Bob was obviously enjoying his company. Much to my surprise, the one I was with seemed to be enjoying my company as well.

We'd read about the "hippie" coffee shops in Greenwich Village, so we suggested that we would go there to further impress the girls. We went into a coffee shop and sat down. The hippie-looking waiter came over and asked me what I wanted.

I didn't drink coffee, but I figured if I ordered a Coke, that might blow the whole thing. So I said, "I'll just have a cup of coffee."

The waiter sneered and asked, "What kind?" while simultaneously pointing to the menu.

Once again, I felt that if I looked at the menu, it might jeopardize my tenuous position. I smiled and said, "Maxwell House."

The girls and the waiter laughed quite a bit. Bob didn't, and neither did I.

I looked at the menu and saw that there were about twenty different kinds of coffees listed, none of which were Maxwell House. Most of them had foreign words in front of them that I didn't understand.

The rest of our evening was spent separately. Bob thought he had a better chance with his young lady if I wasn't around. They went their own way, and my friend and I sat in the coffee shop. We were having an interesting conversation, but neither of us wanted more coffee. She suggested we go to my hotel room, which filled me with what turned out to be false expectations.

We did have a wonderful evening talking, with a little of what was called petting in those days, but we didn't go further than that. And that was quite all right. We were enjoying each other's company and agreed that we'd meet again sometime, either in her hometown of Burlington, Vermont, or maybe she'd come down to Fort Devens. I walked her back to her hotel and kissed her good night, which ultimately turned out to be goodbye, and returned to my room.

Shortly after I got back, Bob was pounding on the door. I opened it, and he came in looking not as dapper as he normally did. I asked him what went wrong.

He said, "You mean, after you?"

Then I answered with another question: "Okay, after me, what went wrong?"

Then he said, "We went to another bar, and after one drink, she suddenly lost interest and left."

Why, he didn't know, but he had his suspicions. He also had no idea what the bar bill was, and by the time he paid it, he'd used up almost all of his money.

He *did* have enough left to take the subway, which was something he'd always wanted to do, anyway. He got on the subway and headed toward Harlem and promptly fell asleep. When he woke up, he wasn't sure where he was and decided to go back to where he started. He jumped down and crossed the tracks to take the next train back. This accounted for the dirt and grease on his hands and clothes.

I asked, "Were you careful around the third rail?"

He looked at me and asked, "What third rail?"

I explained to him that subways ran on electricity, and one rail was electric and dangerous to touch.

He said, "Now you tell me."

We only had a two-day pass, and it was almost a six hour drive back to Fort Devens. We arranged to meet the two other guys between 2:30 and 3:00 at our hotel. After breakfast the next morning, I suggested that we act like the tourists we were and see a little of the city. I enjoyed it, and although Bob tried to look bored, I believe he liked it, too.

On the way back to Fort Devens, Bob's car lost its generator. It got dark about 7:30, which meant we had to drive the last forty or fifty miles in the dark. It started to drizzle, and the windshield wipers wouldn't work without the generator. Our only choice was to stick our heads out the windows. I don't know how we made it, but we did. My first time in New York City was a great adventure for me, and it's still a fond memory. I can't speak for Bob.

Bob and I were firemen for about four weeks when we were notified that we were to report to the sergeant who'd appointed us. We went into his office, and two other firemen were also there. He said he was forced to change our schedules, because our company lost a couple of firemen. There wasn't enough time to replace them before we all shipped out to our new duty stations. The new schedule was one day on and one day off. There would be no more three days off.

When we left his office, I expressed to the other three guys that I was going to quit being a fireman. One of them asked me whether I thought that was an option. I told him I was going to find out. I asked if anyone else was interested in quitting. Bob and John said they also wanted to quit. We went into the sergeant's office and told him our decisions.

Apparently, quitting *was* an option, but not one that the sergeant found to his liking. He yelled at the three of us; and challenged our masculinity, integrity, pedigree, and sanity. He apparently thought we were all hard of hearing, because he screamed at the top of his lungs, even though he was only standing about three feet from us. When he finished yelling, he glared at each of us and referred to us as a slang word for the female genitalia. He asked if we were still quitting. Bob and John said they would stay. I told him I was still going to quit. He then kicked them out, told me to stay, and once we were alone, started laughing.

He looked at me and asked, "Aren't you afraid I'm going to make your life miserable?"

I said, "I think you probably are, but I don't like to be treated unfairly, and this new schedule is unfair."

I told him that ever since I was young, my father had instilled in me the belief that I had to look out for myself and my own best interests.

"When someone challenges my integrity," I said, "I'm convinced that I should stick to my decisions. To back down because you yelled at me or called me names would be giving in to bullying, and I hate bullying."

The sergeant looked at me for a while and asked, "Son, you do know you're in the Army, right?"

"Yes, Sergeant, I do," I said.

"When is your enlistment up?" he asked in a surprisingly compassionate tone.

I said, "In two and a half years, Sergeant."

"I don't think you're going to make it. Now get the hell out of my office."

Which I did.

Bob and I were leaving for Detroit in two weeks, and then on to the Army Language School. During those two weeks, Bob remained a fireman, and I went back to my malingering. The sergeant never punished me, but he taught me a lesson. I learned that when you're in the Army, you're entitled to stand up for yourself as long as you're willing to take the punishment. If you cried or complained, you got punished. It's like playing poker: if you gamble and win, you get to keep the money, but if you lose, you must pay up without complaints. Of course, the question is how important the issue is to you, and is the gamble worth it?

One of my father's favorite poems was "I Sing of Olaf" by E.E. Cummings. It's about a conscientious objector whom Cummings met in the Army during World War I while the poet was stationed at Fort (then Camp) Devens. Olaf put up with weeks of harassment from an officer and other sergeants without giving in. He constantly repeated, "There is some shit I will not eat." Ultimately, they broke Olaf and he died in prison.

In trying to teach me to stand up for myself, my father warned me that those who claim they're eating crap because they have no choice, most often—either consciously or subconsciously—become just like their oppressors. Or, as my father put it, "If you eat shit often enough, you develop a taste for it."

When I was in the Army, I was undoubtedly too naive and too self-centered in my determination of what I would or would not put up with. As I got older, I learned how to choose more worthy battles, but I still believe that my father was right. I've heard many people say that they were putting up with injustices now in order to gain enough power to change things later. My father also said that nobody changes the rules of a game once they start winning.

Bob and I were scheduled to leave Fort Devens on a Monday. On Friday, at the 5:00 p.m. formation, the lieutenant dismissed the company and gave everyone a forty-eight-hour pass, except me. He told me that I had to report to him at 0700 hours the next morning. When I got there, he was with the sergeant who was in charge of the furnaces. The lieutenant asked me if I knew why I didn't get a pass when everyone else did. I told him I thought so. He didn't ask what I thought, but went on to explain that in the three months I'd been there, I'd gotten away with murder. Consequently, he and the sergeant felt that it was time I did a little work. I was going to "GI" the barracks on Saturday and Sunday, which meant sweeping and mopping the floors, applying wax, and buffing.

Each of the two barracks had two floors and a five-foot-wide black linoleum strip down the middle of each floor. The black strip was the only part that had to be waxed and buffed. For reasons known only to the Army, sergeants and officers were allowed to walk on that strip, but no one else. The only time the rest of us were allowed to walk on it was when we were buffing it. We had to walk on either side of the strip, and woe to those who forgot and got caught.

While I was sweeping, waxing, and buffing, the sergeant and the lieutenant were drinking beer. Every once in a while, they'd comment on the job I was doing. The comments were never favorable or flattering, and they always had very little to do with the job I was actually performing. They challenged my ancestry, my masculinity, and my overall worth as a human being. Even *I* realized that this was one time I had to keep my mouth shut, which I did. I finished both barracks late Saturday afternoon. Before dismissing me, the lieutenant said that I didn't have to show up on Sunday, but I *did* have to stay on base. He wished me luck and predicted that I was going to have a good time at the Language School. He also predicted that I'd never get above the rank of E-4, no matter how long I stayed in the Army or how long the Army let me stay. Then he gave me a beer.

On Monday morning, Bob and I left Fort Devens in his Plymouth with a full tank of gas and about $250 each in our pockets for our travel allowance. The Army was allowing us a two-week furlough, plus two weeks to get to California. Our plan was to drive to Detroit and stay there over Christmas and New Year's. Then we'd drive to California, arriving at the Language School on a Friday or Saturday, to report in on the first Monday of January 1958.

Las Vegas, Nevada

Bob and I left Detroit on Wednesday, intending to drive to Ohio and then west until we picked up Route 66. We wanted to drive straight through. We met a friend of a friend in Birmingham, Michigan, who was going out to San Diego. He was stationed at a naval base and agreed to help pay part of the cost of the journey.

A three-day road trip may have been exciting and interesting to Jack Kerouac, but I found it tedious. I would rather drive a car than ride in one, but I wasn't capable of driving for three straight days. We would each drive for six hours and then sleep as much as we could for the next twelve. Bob and I wanted to stop in Las Vegas, which turned out to be an interesting adventure. Our sailor friend took a bus from Vegas to San Diego.

This was 1958, and Las Vegas was still a new town. There were a number of casinos in what is now the downtown area of Vegas, but only one casino on what was known as the Strip.

Bob and I considered ourselves decent blackjack players, but we stayed away from the slots and the crap tables. We both had about $75 left from our travel pay. Las Vegas, at that time, was an inexpensive city to stay in—if you didn't gamble. Our hotel room was modest and cheap, and you could buy a meal ticket in the large casinos that would allow you to go into the buffet room and eat whatever you wanted. I believe the meal tickets for the entire day were about $3. You could drink for free if you were gambling, and they didn't ask for ID.

Once we learned the rules of Vegas blackjack etiquette (no talking, scratching with a card for a hit, or waving your hand over your card to stay), our playing started off well. Bob was up about $100, and I was up a little less than that. I think we both thought we'd found a system that worked for us.

I was confident that we were going to walk out of Vegas with a lot of money. At one point, I went to the bathroom, and there was a shoeshine guy in there who just ran his brush over my shoes a couple of times. I gave him a $10 chip. Walking out the door, I realized that was a fairly generous tip for a soldier who was earning $72 a month, but Vegas was like Never, Never Land. There was no sense of time, and money takes on a kind of make-believe essence. You're using chips, and they're all the same size, but different denominations. I don't think I ever had a $50 bill in my hand in my life, but at one point, I was holding three $50 chips.

On the second day, Bob and I hit a bad spell. We were down to about $40 each. We stopped playing for a while, because the dealer, when he wasn't getting blackjack, was hitting fifteen and sixteen and winning with twenty or twenty-one We decided to try a new dealer. In a very short time, we were both back up, each winning about $100.

Being young, foolish, and competitive, we went back to the dealer who'd been beating us and promptly lost all of our money again. We decided to leave that day anyway, so we put our last change together and played the slots. We lost.

We left Vegas and drove to Monterey, using my father's gasoline credit card. He'd loaned it to me just in case of emergency. We filled up Bob's Plymouth with gas, which cost $5. We asked if the cashier could put $10 on the credit card and give us $5. He did, and we lived on that money until we got to Monterey, with about seventy-five cents to last us until payday, which was, thank goodness, the next day.

I hurriedly sent a letter to my father, saying that the credit card he'd lent me in case of an emergency had come in very handy. I failed to explain the details of the emergency, but I did tell him to expect a larger-than-usual bill the following month.

☆ ☆ ☆

CHAPTER 3

Six Months at the Army Language School

Monterey, California

When we arrived in Monterey, Bob and I reported to the Language School. Bob was assigned to the Russian barracks, which were old, wooden buildings similar to the kind we had at Fort Lewis and Fort Devens. I was assigned to a room in a new brick building on top of a hill, which housed all the German, French, and Spanish students. Our view overlooked the Monterey Bay. I had a desk, a bed, and a closet. I also had a roommate, Bill O'Hara, who was from Boston and a graduate of Holy Cross University. He was three years older than I was and a literature and philosophy major.

Our first weekend in Monterey was right out of a movie. We met two girls in a bar, who took us to a party in town on Saturday night. We had a good time together, so they invited us to the last day of the Bing Crosby golf tournament at Pebble Beach, which was on Sunday. It turned out that their parents were both members of Del Monte Lodge, and the girls had tickets for the tournament, which also allowed them to bring guests into the lounge. Bob and

I found ourselves walking around this beautiful golf course with its magnificent clubhouse, filled with people we'd seen in movies, heard on the radio, and read about. For a couple of nineteen-year-old boys from Detroit, it was quite a heady experience.

That night, we found ourselves drinking at the bar with Bob Hope, Bing Crosby, Phil Harris, and a young Ken Venturi. To say we were drinking with these gentlemen is a bit of an exaggeration, because we were at one end of the bar with our dates, and they were at the far end of the bar, surrounded by their friends. Regardless, we were at the same bar, and we were all drinking.

A friend of mine named Don Saville was in the Seabees and stationed on the island of Guam. A USO troupe visited Guam to entertain the sailors, and one of the entertainers was Kathy Grant, who later became Bing Crosby's wife. Saville told me he was so impressed with her that he followed the USO troupe back to the airport and got on the plane she was on. As it happened, there was about a two-hour delay, and Saville was able to engage Kathy in a nice conversation. He said they actually took a walk together along a nearby beach. He wasn't known as someone who lied or even stretched the truth, but most of us found the story difficult to believe, probably because we were envious.

Saville was good-looking, but as far as we were concerned, not good-looking enough to attract Kathy Grant. While following the golf tournament, I happened to see her walking by herself. She was now Kathy Crosby, and Bing was nearby, but I still felt I needed to check out Saville's story.

I approached her, apologized, and asked if I could ask her a question. She smiled and said, "Okay."

I told her the story that Saville had told me, without mentioning his name. I also told her that I bet him $10 that the story wasn't true.

She looked at me and said, "If the young man's name is Don Saville, you owe him $10."

She then introduced me to Bing Crosby, who was standing nearby, and actually said, "This is a friend of Don Saville, the young Seabee I met on Guam."

The next week, I wrote a letter to Saville and enclosed a money order for $10 and an apology. I found Bob and the girls and told them the story. We then went into a bar to spend the rest of the day and part of the night with our newfound drinking buddies.

☆ ☆ ☆

My roommate and I were both German students, and we had to report to class at 8:00 a.m. There were sixty German students total, who were divided into classes of seven or eight students. Each class contained one officer, and the rest were enlisted men. The officer in my class was named Karl Weber. He was a warrant officer who was assigned to Army Intelligence. He was in his early forties and married. His ancestry was German, but he never spoke the language. He was drafted into the Army during World War II and fought throughout Europe. He was with the first American group in Berlin at the end of the war, and they also liberated a concentration camp.

Warrant Officer Weber liked me, and warrant officers are allowed to associate with enlisted men, whereas the other officers cannot. We became friends, and he told me many stories about his experiences during the war, most of which were salacious, humorous, or horrendous.

On the first day of school, we were sitting in the classroom when a very tall, ramrod-straight gentleman with a missing left arm walked into the room. He stood behind a rather large and heavy-looking oak table, and proceeded to reach down and move it with his one arm, which certainly got our attention. He then approached me, and from a distance of about four feet, looked me in the eyes and asked, "Sind sie schüler heir?"

I looked at him dumbfounded and sat silently. He moved a little closer and said a little louder, "Sind sie schüler heir?"

I looked around the classroom for help, but everybody was looking down, so I looked back at this one-armed man, and through his glasses, I was able to see his icy blue eyes that were completely devoid of empathy. I concluded he wasn't going to help me either.

He then got about two feet from my face and said in a voice that would have made a drill sergeant proud, "Sind sie schüler heir?"

I looked back at him and said, as best I could, "Zent sie schuler heir."

He smiled, patted me on my head, and repeated that exercise with the student next to me. After he'd gone through all eight of us, he stood in front of the class and waved his one arm like a symphony conductor. "Sind sie schüler heir?"

We all responded as best as we could, "Zent sie shuler heir." We didn't know that his question meant, "Are you a student here?" but we did know that the one-armed man didn't care whether we understood. What he wanted was for us to repeat after him.

That was our introduction to the Army Language School's method of total immersion. Every day, six German teachers would come into the room. Each teacher would speak to us in simple German sentences that we had to repeat without knowing what they meant. The teachers tried to have each of us repeat the words as they spoke them. They would correct certain sounds that we repeated incorrectly. Some of us were better able to duplicate the teacher's pronunciation than others. Those students with musical backgrounds and/or close to perfect pitch were able to pick up the proper pronunciation the quickest. Most of us were never able to repeat the sounds exactly, but we could come close, which was good enough for our teachers.

Our instructors never used English while teaching us German, but there were a few times when they explained the Language School method to us in English. One such incident had to do with accents. They told us that everyone who learns another language before the age of thirteen or fourteen has a better chance of speaking without an accent. We're all born with enough facial muscles to speak every language we hear growing up, but we don't use all the muscles we have. We only use the ones we need. By fourteen, the muscles we don't use will atrophy, and we have to use different muscles for a new language. The result is a slight to severe accent. Most other countries start foreign-language learning in elementary school for that reason.

When I was in Germany, I was told that I spoke German with a Scandinavian accent, which was a compliment. The American accent is often used for comic relief in German movies. I have no idea why I would have a Scandinavian accent. My mother's parents came from Sweden, and my grandmother lived with us until I was fifteen, but I never learned or attempted to learn Swedish.

Within a few days, we figured out what some of the words meant, but we still had to repeat sentences that we memorized in the same way an opera singer might memorize words to an aria in a foreign language. During our breaks and after school, we all voiced our frustration with the method.

When not in classes, we could talk to some of the teachers. We asked them if we were ever going to hear English in the classroom. They said no; however, as a result of our insistence, they allowed us, after the third or fourth week, to have one hour in which we could ask the instructors questions. By that point, most of us had figured out the basic grammar rules, but we needed to know certain things that didn't make sense to us.

I remember that one of the first questions was about the many ways Germans say the word *The*. We were told that *Der* was masculine, *Die* was feminine, and *Das* was neuter. The follow-up question was:

"How do you know whether a word is masculine, feminine, or neuter?"

They said there was little rhyme or reason, and only a few rules that one could learn. For the most part, that aspect of German had to be memorized until one developed a feel for the language.

After I was in Germany for a year or so, I found out that geography played a role in determining the gender of a German noun. The word *Coca-Cola* in northern Germany was feminine, or *die Coca-Cola*; while in southern Germany, it was *das Coca-Cola*. I even heard it called *der Coca-Cola* in some areas.

After our one-hour session, some of us had a better understanding of German grammar, but there was still a great deal of confusion. It became a matter of faith that things would become clearer as we went along.

☆ ☆ ☆

We were told that the proper way to address a warrant officer was *Mister*. One Friday afternoon, Mr. Weber asked me if I would meet him at the Mission Ranch in Carmel for a drink. I met him at 8:30

p.m., and we had a couple of drinks with dinner. Afterward, he asked me if I'd do him a favor. He said he was going to meet a lady friend and would be with her until midnight.

He said, "If my wife asks you, tell her I was here with you until 1:00 a.m."

I'd met Mrs. Weber the week before in a restaurant where they both were having lunch. She invited me to attend her husband's birthday party, which was in two weeks' time, and I accepted.

I wasn't a prude, but in my neighborhood, we had certain rules regarding relationships with women. If a friend of ours was dating a girl, no one would ever ask that girl out. Nor would they make a move on her at a party. It was almost never done. In fact, if our friend broke up with his girl and someone wanted to take her out, they would ask him if that was all right. If he said no, then they wouldn't take her out.

When Mr. Weber explained to me that I was going to be his alibi, I felt a little conflicted. That was what I called cheating, whether you were married or just going with a girl. I believed that cheating was wrong and unfair. I didn't know how to say that to Mr. Weber, so I went along with what he suggested. I think he could tell that this wasn't exactly what I wanted to do, so he explained his position. He told me that he loved his wife very much and had no desire to divorce her, but he said that he didn't get married until he was in his mid-thirties, and prior to that, he'd had numerous girlfriends. He said he struggled with the idea of cheating on his wife, and decided that all men are dogs. He felt that men weren't capable of controlling certain desires.

I listened to him, and although I respected him, I didn't buy his explanation. I wasn't willing to go along with his theory. I didn't believe that my father was a dog, I knew my brother wasn't a dog, and I hoped that *I* wasn't a dog. I did agree to be his alibi, though, and silently hoped that his wife would never question me, because I was also very much opposed to lying.

My father had once told me that he'd given me as much freedom as he did when I was a teenager, because he didn't want me to have to lie. He wasn't religious, but he said he believed in two commandments:

(1) Be as honest as possible with everyone, including yourself; and

(2) never intentionally hurt someone. He said we hurt people all the time accidentally, but to do so intentionally was bullying. I've always appreciated that and have tried to live by those rules.

As Mr. Weber left, he handed me a $20 bill.

He said, "I don't expect you to spend your own money doing me this favor."

I protested, ever so slightly, to no avail, as $20 was a lot of money to a soldier who was making $72 a month.

Mr. Weber also asked me to bring along Bob to his birthday party. He told me that there would be officers there, so if anyone were to ask, we were to say we were officers. This was another request that made me nervous. Luckily, no one asked.

For Bob and me, it was an interesting experience. Mr. Weber's wife was from a very wealthy and genteel southern family. There were numerous glasses, plates, and a variety of spoons, forks, and knives on the dinner table. We both had to take cues from those who were sitting next to us as to how to use these utensils. The food was fantastic, but for me, anything other than peanut butter and jelly was new and exotic.

After dinner, everyone had a few more drinks. One couple who'd been stationed in Korea said that they wanted to do a song and dance for us that they'd learned while over there. They sang in a high-pitched, sing-song fashion while doing a dance that mimicked shoveling coal. Bob and I found it rather embarrassing to watch an officer act so foolishly.

A few weeks later, we had a general inspection. I was in the front line and noticed that one of the inspecting officers was the lieutenant who'd sung the Korean coal miner's song from Mr. Weber's dinner. As he approached me, I knew I was going to have a difficult time keeping a straight face. When he got in front of me, he inspected my uniform and then looked me in the eyes. I wasn't laughing, but I was smiling. Just before he was going to ask me why I was smiling, it must have dawned on him where he'd seen me before. I could almost feel his embarrassment. I don't know if he ever asked Warrant Officer Weber about it, but I doubt it.

All members of the ASA had to have security clearances. When we joined, we filled out forms that were sent to the FBI for investigation. Among other things, we had to list five personal and three professional references. I didn't know it then, but I later found out that the FBI investigated the references and the neighbors or co-workers of those references.

One of my professional references was my former boss at Ford Motor Company, where I worked for nine months before going to college. He was a huge man, aptly named Al Samson. I felt he liked me, but I wasn't positive. I included his name because the only professional references I had were teachers, and I was more concerned about what they might say.

I went to visit him on that same leave and felt a little trepidation. He seemed happy to see me, and when I asked him about any visits from the FBI, he laughed and said:

"What a sanctimonious asshole. He slithered into the outer office, ignored my secretary, and came into my office announcing that he was from the FBI and showed me his badge. I stood up and told him I was a commander in the U.S. Naval Reserve. Then I ordered him to report the nature of his visit to my secretary. When Jackie told me he was here about you, I let him back in. He asked all the formal questions and then asked if there was anything 'special' I wanted to add. I was going to ask, 'You mean is he a closet homo?' as a joke, but I thought better of it. He was so uptight that he probably didn't understand jokes."

The second Friday night of our stay at the Language School, Bob and I tested our false IDs. We had three pieces of proof that stated our ages as twenty-three for me and twenty-two for Bob. We got the proof while we were in college for that one misspent year, and it was accepted by all the bars that we tried in Michigan. We also used the proof in Boston with no problem, which always surprised me. I was a skinny, brown-haired kid who didn't shave. Even after the Army in my first year of teaching, when I was twenty-six, I was often mistaken for a student. I was eighteen when I got the proof, and I used it successfully until I turned twenty-one. My only explanation was that the bartenders must have figured, anyone looking as young as I did, would be foolish to try using a fake ID.

My first piece of proof was a draft card. A friend gave it to me, and I never asked where he got it. The name on it was Kermit McDonald, born on April 19, 1934. I wasn't ever going into any bar with a name like Kermit, so I carefully erased it and typed in Gerald, thereby killing two birds with one stone. I disliked my real first name, Gerard, as much as I disliked Kermit.

My second piece of proof was a hospital birth certificate. It was what the hospital sent to the state, who then issued an official birth certificate. I filled it out and stamped it with a notary's seal I got from another friend.

The third piece was an application for a New York State driver's license. Another friend said they were available in any New York State Social Security office. He picked up a few and gave them to his friends in Detroit. I also got a Social Security card made out to Gerald McDonald that anyone could get. It wasn't a valid piece of identification, but sometimes a clever bartender wouldn't even look at someone's proof. Instead, he'd place his hand over the proof and ask for anything else with your name on it. That worked whenever the underage person was using some older person's ID.

Bob and I went to downtown Monterey and into the first bar we saw on the main street. Our ID was accepted with no problem. We then went into three more bars. One bartender told us he knew we were from Michigan before he even looked at our ID. I asked him how he knew. He said because we produced three pieces of identification. He was from Michigan, and he said only in that state did they demand three pieces of proof.

In the last bar we went into, there was an attractive young woman playing the piano. We stayed there, seated around the piano, for about forty-five minutes. As we were leaving, I mentioned to

Bob that there were no women in the bar. We hadn't noticed the name of the bar, which was The Gilded Cage. We decided that it might be a gay bar, but thought nothing of it.

On Monday when I arrived to class at 8:00 a.m., Warrant Officer Weber approached me and asked what Bob and I were doing at The Gilded Cage. I asked him how he knew that.

He said, "I'm with Military Intelligence. I thought you knew that."

He then said, "Your name was on a list, along with Bob's, which could lead to the removal of your security clearances."

I must've blanched, because he said, "Don't worry. I took your names off the list."

I asked him if he was serious, and he said, "Yes. You could've easily lost your clearances."

I protested, "That's not even close to fair. They should at least tell us which bars are off limits."

He smiled and said, "The Army isn't interested in being fair. Not only would they have dropped your clearances, but they would also never have explained why. You would have been informed that you no longer had a clearance and would be transferred out of the Language School. You would've probably ended up as a truck driver."

That was another important lesson for me. Not only did we have to play by the Army rules, but we also had to anticipate how the Army might think about something.

The next Friday night, after school was over, Bob and I drove the ten miles from Monterey to downtown Carmel. We both realized instantly that this was where we wanted to spend our free time. Carmel was not only beautiful, but it was filled with interesting, artistic, attractive people, a good portion of whom were women. We came back on Saturday and looked around for a house we could afford to rent there. We found one on Torres Street, which is at the bottom of the hill that led to downtown. We were told that the home had previously been rented by Bing Crosby's twin sons when they were stationed at Fort Ord. It was $100 a month. We said that we'd be right back with the first two months' rent.

We borrowed the money from a couple of Army friends, who each loaned us $50. I got the other $100 from Mr. Weber, who thought a place in Carmel would be exactly what Bob and I needed. The guy who lent me $50 said that he'd be interested in living there also, if we were looking for more roommates. It was a small, two-bedroom, one-bath house with a living room, a dining room, and a small kitchen. It had a sofa bed in the living room, and we thought we could put a mattress on the floor in the dining room, and get two more roommates. Bob and I figured we could afford no more than $25 a month.

The guy who loaned me $50 was from Denver, Colorado. His name was Meyer, and he had a brand-new Ford convertible. He'd attended an Eastern prep school and spent two years at Yale. He was a tall, clean-cut guy who must've stood out back East with his brush cut, Levi's, and cowboy boots. I met him briefly at Fort Devens when we were waiting to ship out. I liked him, and he was very smart. In fact, he ended up number one in our German class. Bob and I were both thrilled to have him as a roommate.

Our fourth roommate was Doug Marks, a young man from a small town in Michigan. He met us at Fort Devens and wanted to experience the wildlife. Bob was probably the wildest person he'd ever met.

I don't remember how it was determined, but I had one bedroom and David had the other. Doug slept on the living room sofa, and Bob used a mattress on the floor in the dining room. We all shared the closets, the cleaning, and the cooking, which was primarily opening beer cans.

We quickly developed a pattern of Friday night partying on the beach with the purpose of meeting college or local females. We'd invite them back to our house under the condition that they bring their own beer, as well as some for us. David didn't drink beer; he drank Scotch. He knew a number of students who went to Stanford, whom he invited down the third weekend that we were in the house. This led to an exciting and almost deadly adventure.

David's friends arrived on Saturday morning and brought with them a girl who played the guitar and sang folk songs. She told us that she played in a bar in San Francisco called The Hungry I. She said that she was friends with the group that played there, known as The Kingston Trio. She had an album with her that the trio had just produced called, *The Kingston Trio at the Hungry I*. We all listened to it and loved every song. She sang a few songs of her own, one of which I'll never forget. It was an old folk song called "Delia's Gone." There are various versions to the song, as well as the story behind the song. I don't remember her rendition, but I do remember being totally enchanted by her singing.

The following weekend, they asked if they could come back. They were going to bring some truck inner tubes so we could all raft down the Carmel River, which sounded fantastic. We gathered at a spot on the river that would allow us to launch our inner tubes. We drove the truck about ten miles down the river and left it there.

We all got on top of our inner tubes and started drifting slowly down the placid river. There were about ten of us in individual tubes. The young lady with the guitar was in one, and luckily, she decided at the last minute not to bring her guitar with her. We had bags of beer that we tied to the inner tubes. I had on my prescription sunglasses, and we all floated gently down the Carmel River. After a few minutes, we made a turn in the river and ran into some very small rapids. I remember saying, "This is terrific."

We then approached another turn and some much larger rapids. I said, "Oh, shit!"

The girl next to me was knocked out of her inner tube and went under. I reached for her and fell out of *my* tube. I grabbed on to a tree that was embedded in the middle of the river and pushed the girl toward shore. She made it there, along with three or four other people. They yelled that I should push off from the tree toward shore, and they'd grab my hand.

"I can't do that, because I have to find my sunglasses," I said.

They yelled, "How do you expect to do that?"

I was perfectly sober and said, "I'll just wait till all the water rushes by."

They all started laughing. It took me a while to realize just how stupid that comment was. After I regained my senses, I told them that I was going to launch myself toward them and try to grab their hands. I pushed off, but the water was too swift. It took me downriver and underwater. When I came up, I saw some branches hanging from a bush on the shore. I grabbed them and started to pull myself in. It was only after I reached shore that I realized that both my hands and parts of my body were cut by the thorns on the branches. I didn't care. I was extremely grateful to be out of that river.

All of us escaped safely. We were told that if we'd made it a little farther down, we would've been in great jeopardy. The river was filled with debris from a previous storm, and the locals knew not to attempt any rafting.

Like many foolish young people, we celebrated our escape from death by illegally climbing over the wall of the venerable Carmel Mission and getting pleasantly drunk while trespassing in the courtyard of that beautiful old church, listening to folk songs.

One of the couples who came the next weekend from Stanford were friends of David's. Their names were Jerry and Carol. David gave them his bedroom. Sunday, around noon, when they were about to leave, I went into David's room and saw that it was in shambles.

I went into the living room, approached Carol, and said, "It's customary here for our guests to leave the room the way they found it."

She looked at me, astounded, and said, "You expect me to clean that room?"

I smiled and said, "If you're the one who messed it up, why wouldn't you clean it?"

She said, "I don't clean."

Jerry volunteered to clean the room, but I stopped him. I told him that would set a bad precedent, and said, "The rule here is whoever messes up the room, cleans the room. The two of you were in there, and the two of you have to clean it."

Carol stomped off to the room and came out about half an hour later, still angry. Jerry came out somewhat sheepish looking. I went in, and the room met with my approval. Sgt. Eagle would have been proud.

After they left, David told me that Carol's father was a high-ranking attorney in Eisenhower's attorney general office. He laughed and said he assumed she'd never cleaned anything in her life. He was so glad that I'd insisted.

One day, David asked me if I wanted to go on a double date. I said, "Sure, who are the girls?"

He said they were family friends who lived in Los Angeles. I looked at him and asked, "What time do we have to leave?"

"About noon," he said. "It's a five-hour drive, and we're expected for dinner. The girls have just graduated from high school, and the family is having a private party for them and some of their friends. The girls thought it would be fun to have a couple of older guys as dates."

We left about 12:30 on Friday and drove down Highway 101, which was a beautiful drive for me, but had to be harrowing for David. He could never take his eyes off the road because of all the twists and turns, but I was able to gaze at the beauty that is Big Sur, and the rest of that stretch all the way down to Los Angeles. I slept through some of the last part of the trip, because David would never let anyone drive his car. He woke me when we reached the outskirts of L.A. I remember being somewhat confused, because not far from the sign that said, "Los Angeles city limits" was another sign that said, "42 miles to Los Angeles." David pointed out that L.A. was quite a large city.

When we arrived at the house, which was larger than any home I'd ever seen up close, I was introduced to Carol, who was David's date, and to her parents. They escorted David and me to our rooms. Each of us had our own bedroom with our own attached bathroom.

I said to myself, "This is the way I want to be able to treat my guests when I grow up."

I'd grown up on a street called Roselawn, which is on the West Side of Detroit. We had a number of overnight and weekly guests, mostly relatives, but they slept in a room in our attic and shared the one bath that was on the first floor. This was certainly different.

We changed our clothes and went down to the dining room for dinner, which also turned out to be something I'd never experienced before. I felt very self-conscious, because of all the silverware that was on the table. I felt there were way too many knives, forks, spoons, glasses, and plates for six people. I tried to take all my cues from David, because I knew he was used to all of this, and I lived in fear that it would become painfully obvious to everyone else that I wasn't.

After dinner, we dressed for the party, which was at the home of my date, whose name was Lisa. It was held outside, around an enormous swimming pool. We got there about 8:30, and the other guests started arriving at 9:00. Almost all the guests were underage, but there were servants serving them drinks. I smiled to myself and thought that not every underage person in California needs a fake ID.

After drinks and hors d'oeuvres were served, the entertainment arrived. It was Andre Previn at the piano and Shelly Manne on the drums. My musical tastes were still fairly limited, but I'd been exposed to some jazz, and I recognized both of their names.

I don't know what David had told Lisa, but she seemed to know or sense that I was somewhat uncomfortable. She tried very hard to make me relax. I limited myself to one drink, which helped. I didn't want to get drunk and make an even bigger fool out of myself than I was afraid was going to happen, anyway.

The party was rather sedate compared to what I was used to in Detroit, and I enjoyed it. The young people were friendly and asked David and me about the Army Language School. We managed to instill a certain sense of mystery into our explanation by telling them we were in Army Intelligence and were forbidden to talk about what we did.

The party started to break up about midnight, and the girls said they wanted some Mexican food. We all got into the car, and David asked, "Where to?"

Carol said her favorite Mexican restaurant was right over the border in Tijuana. I didn't know much about Tijuana, other than that it was in Mexico, but I figured it was far enough away that she had to be joking. I was wrong. Tijuana was about 150 miles away. When we got there, after about two and a half hours of driving, we found the restaurant. Everyone ordered food with Spanish names and said I should try this or that because:

"It's the best you'll ever taste."

I knew that was going to be true no matter what I ordered, because I'd never eaten or even heard of anything they mentioned. I didn't want them to know that this was the first time I'd ever been in a Mexican restaurant. I told them I wasn't hungry and just wanted something simple. It appeared that the simplest thing I could order was a beef taco, which I also had never eaten before, but I'd heard of it. Much to my surprise, I enjoyed it. We all had Mexican beers, and I wondered what the drinking laws were in Mexico, but I assumed that underage drinking was not a major concern in this border town.

We drove back to L.A., and the girls wanted to swim. I assumed that since the city was near the water, swimming wouldn't include a long drive. I was wrong again. They wanted to go to a particular beach that was about an hour and a half away. I didn't have swim trunks, and I didn't think anyone else did, either. So far, the evening had been interesting and fun, but no hanky-panky. I thought skinny-dipping might change all that.

When we arrived at the beach, David handed me some swim trunks. The girls had suits on underneath their dresses, which indicated that everyone knew the evening would include swimming, except me. It turned out to be fun, even without any hanky-panky.

After we'd had enough swimming, we drove back to their house, and David suggested we have a nightcap. I had one small Scotch on the rocks, and I don't remember what Lisa had, but I think she was still drinking beer. What I do remember is that she lit a fire in the fireplace, and we all laid down on this beautiful, soft rug. As we listened to the crackling of the fire, Lisa leaned close to me and whispered, "Thank you for a lovely evening."

Then she gave a long kiss that I thought might lead to something. She nestled close to me, which was another promising sign, and was asleep in about two minutes. It wasn't exactly what I'd had in mind, but it was the end of a fascinating adventure.

The next day, David and I got up around 10:00 a.m. We had a great breakfast with the family and left to go back to Monterey about noon. That was my first exposure to a lifestyle I'd only seen in the movies, and I hoped I would see it again.

☆ ☆ ☆

David and I liked to get to school early. We would leave in his car, and Bob and Doug would drive later in Bob's car. This drive revealed an interesting aspect of David's personality. He charged me a dollar a day for gas. I was used to chipping in for gas money with my friends at home. I knew, and he knew I knew, that he didn't need the money. He also knew that $5 a week was a big deal for me, so one day I asked him why he was doing it.

He said, "If I don't, I won't know if you're my friend because you like me, or because you like my money. This is one reason why wealthy people hang around with other wealthy people."

I was hurt. "You really think I like you for your money?"

He hesitated a moment, "No, but I need to be certain."

I looked at him and asked, "You wouldn't charge a hitchhiker for gas money, would you?"

"Of course not," he answered.

I said, "Then just think of me as a hitchhiker who just happens to be headed your way every weekday."

"Nice try, but I'm not buying that," he said.

"How about if I sign a statement proclaiming my friendship in blood?" I asked.

He laughed and told me that he'd think it over.

After that discussion, I would give David $5 a week whenever he asked for it, but most of the time he didn't ask.

The first three months of instruction were very difficult. The Language School method is effective, but it's not easy. We had to memorize two pages of dialogue every morning, and each of the students in my class had to recite those two pages from memory in front of the whole class.

All of our German instructors, except one woman, were former officers in the German Army during World War II. One of them was on the general's staff. They all had a very direct way of correcting any mistakes we made. Some students took those corrections, and the manner in which they were given, as personal affronts, especially my roommate, Bill.

I spent most of my evenings in Carmel at our house on Torres Street. I would drive back with David in the morning, and he and I would study the dialogue on our way to school. I would then go over it a couple more times before and after breakfast. We were told that the best way to learn the dialogue was to read it out loud just before we went to bed and to do it again two or three times in the morning.

I always had a good memory, and I found learning the dialogue relatively easy. If I made a mistake, I'd try to improvise, which even the German instructors found somewhat amusing. My roommate from Holy Cross had an extremely difficult time with the dialogue, and if he got stuck, he'd stand there and stutter. It was sad to watch. Usually he just sat back down.

One morning after I arrived back to my room and started to prepare for class, Bill was standing there looking somewhat glassy-eyed. He said to me, "You're really going to fail this one. It's very long and very difficult."

He had a kind of demonic smile, as if somehow my impending demise was going to give him a great deal of pleasure. We went to class, and I did stumble a bit, but I was able to successfully finish. I received a pat on the head and a smile from my instructor. Bill made it through the first two lines and then literally crumbled. He couldn't say a word. He looked at the instructor, the one-armed gentleman who'd been a captain in the German Army, and started crying. Our instructor told him he was excused for the day and could go back to his room.

When I showed up to my room the next morning, it appeared as if he hadn't slept.

Bill said to me, "I now know how you do it. You go out every night and drink and sleep with women, and I stay here and study. The only way you could successfully learn those dialogues is if you were getting help from someone. God certainly wouldn't help a drunken womanizer, so I figured it out. You've made a pact with the devil, and I'm going to expose you for what you are."

I didn't know what to do. It was obvious that he was having some type of breakdown, but at nineteen years old, I didn't know what the right course of action for a breakdown was. We had a sergeant on each floor who was supposed to be in command. Ours was Sergeant Stewart, and he was also in the German School, but not in my class. I went to him and told him what was going on with my roommate. We walked back to the room, and the sergeant was able to see immediately that Bill was in trouble. He told me to go to school and that he'd take care of everything.

I learned later that he drove Bill to see a psychiatrist who was at Fort Ord. I never saw my roommate again, and I never found out where he ended up. I did hear from many other students that this wasn't uncommon. The Language School method was intense and stressful. We were encouraged to unwind on the weekends, which Bob and I took to heart, but Bill, unfortunately, didn't or couldn't.

There was one sergeant in his forties who was studying Serbo-Croatian. He complained a few times to a doctor that he couldn't keep up with the younger students. The doctor reminded him that he was a World War II and Korean War combat veteran, and if he could do *that*, he could do anything. He dismissed him and told him not to come back. The next day, the sergeant committed suicide with his bayonet.

After about the third month, the rewards from this grueling method started to kick in. I found myself dreaming in German, and using words in my dreams I didn't think I knew, which I found mystifying. We were also having much more fun with the language. We had a music class where we would learn German songs, usually drinking songs that are sung with bands at the numerous festivals they have in Germany. Soon I knew the words to all of the songs we sang. Our favorite was called, "Die Lorelei." It was a poem by Heinrich Heine, put to music. I even taught the song to Bob, who could sing well and had perfect pitch. In fact, Bob sang in the Russian chorus at the Language School.

Our instructors also took us on excursions, one of which was to a German bar where we had a German lunch that the Army paid for. By the fifth month, many of us were holding small conversations among ourselves in German. The lines that we learned in our dialogues, all of which involved common, everyday experiences, started to become second nature to us. We knew how to order in a restaurant. We knew how to get a haircut. We knew how to ask directions. And we knew every room in a house. We did spend a considerable amount of time learning military vocabulary, which we all knew would be the first words we'd forget, but we needed them for our ASA assignments in Germany.

The longest word we learned was German for "barbed-wire entanglement," which is *stackledrahtverhau*. The Germans have a penchant for putting words together, rather than forming new words. For example, instead of saying that a person loitered, the Germans call it *herumstehen*, which literally means "standing around." One of my favorite German words is *staubsauger*, which literally means "dust sucker," and is their word for "vacuum cleaner."

After six months, our course was finished, and we had a little graduation ceremony. Each of us was relatively fluent in German.

Of the sixty who started, fifty-six finished. I never found out what happened to those who failed, including my roommate, Bill.

I studied Latin in high school and French in my first year of college, but I didn't learn either of those languages; however, I did learn German. I was comfortable in my pronunciation, and I was reasonably fluent with my vocabulary. I had enough words at my disposal so that I could carry on a normal conversation and speak, for the most part, grammatically correct Standard German, which is called *Hoch Deutsch*, or High German.

I felt that the Army did an amazing job of teaching us. Of course, the Army imposed some incentives that a university could not. Classes were small, attendance was mandatory, and skipping class was a court-martial offense. Failure meant being sent to the infantry for the next two and a half years.

There were many advantages to being stationed at the Language School. We were soldiers and wore uniforms, but we were treated more like students. I thought the Language School was in sunny California, but when I arrived, I found out that we had to wear our winter uniforms all year round. The average morning temperature in Monterey was in the low- to high 40s, because of the fog rolling in off of the Pacific Ocean. When or if the skies cleared and the sun came out, the temperature could climb well into the high 70s or low 80s.

The Army determined the uniform for the day by the morning temperatures, which meant that we always had to wear our winter uniforms. When it got warmer in our classrooms, most officers would allow us to remove our jackets and loosen our ties, but there were always a few by-the-book second lieutenants who, if they saw you outside the classroom, would tell you to shape up. But generally speaking, the Language School was like a large, beautiful campus, one block from the ocean.

The Army, being the Army, did feel it was necessary to remind us that we were still government property. They couldn't give us duties during the week, because they wanted us to concentrate on our language learning, but they did assign details on the weekends. Even these details were different from what I experienced in Basic Training and at Fort Devens. Instead of doing the assigned duty yourself, you could pay someone to take your duty for you. I think the going rate was $10. There were also so many soldiers and so few details that on average, each soldier would be assigned a duty once every five or six weeks. When I got assigned to server duty one weekend, I decided to take it, because I had no plans for that weekend and no money. I also wanted to prove something to my comrades.

The Army mess halls were staffed with cooks, enlisted men who were detailed to do KP, and enlisted men who were detailed to serve the food cafeteria-style. This is true on every Army base. For the seventeen months I'd been in the Army, I heard soldiers beg for a second helping of mashed potatoes or more green beans and never receive any. The servers would look at their best friends and say, "Move along, only one serving per trooper," knowing that the next day they were going to be on the other side of the counter doing the begging, and also knowing that the mess sergeants always made more than was eaten and the leftovers were always thrown away.

I told my friends to be sure to eat in the mess hall that Saturday for dinner. They were serving beef for the main dish. The Army always started with top-quality meats and, depending on the skill and dedication of the cooks, the result could be fine dining. I had two of the best Thanksgiving dinners of my life in the Army, which even included excellent wines.

When I showed up for my detail, I was assigned to serve mashed potatoes, but I switched with the guy serving the meat. I told my roommates and classmates to get to the front of the line. As they approached my station, I asked them how many pieces of meat they wanted. Some said, two pieces, and some said three. I'd probably served about fourteen to sixteen friends, when the mess sergeant came rushing over, yelling, "What the fuck are you doing?"

"The troops are hungry, Sergeant." I answered.

He grabbed the serving fork out of my hand, grabbed my arm with his other hand, and marched me over to the front of the line where another soldier was serving little slices of butter.

"Here you go, asshole, serve the butter and give them as much as they want."

I felt I'd made my point, but the next Saturday when I asked the friend who'd received three pieces of tasty roast beef from me if I could have more potatoes, he didn't look up when he said, "Move along, trooper, only one to a customer."

☆ ☆ ☆

Bob knew that when David, Doug, and I left at the end of June, he'd need new roommates. He had one lined up in Jack Webber, who was from Detroit and had joined the Army when Bob and I did. He started Basic Training with us at Fort Lewis, but was injured and sent to a hospital. After his release from the hospital, he finished Basic Training at Fort Ord. He took the Language School test there and was assigned to the yearlong Russian course in the same class Bob was in. Bob and I often wondered why the Army didn't send us to Fort Ord to take the test, rather than across the country to Fort Devens. Maybe it was because it made too much sense.

Jack was a big, strong guy who stood about 6'2" tall and weighed about 200 pounds. He was a couple of years older than I was and had graduated from Michigan State University. Upon graduation, he was eligible for the draft, so he joined the Army. He was already a semi-roommate. He was there most of the time, but he didn't usually sleep over, so it was natural that he would become one of Bob's new roommates.

One day, Bob came to me and said, "I think I found another roommate." He told me that he'd met a member of the newest Russian class who asked him if he knew where he could buy a car. Bob said he drove him to a GM dealership in Monterey, and his new friend bought a brand-new Pontiac convertible and paid cash for it. Bob figured if he could do that, he'd have no trouble paying $25 a month as a roommate.

He also said that this new guy, whose name was Bowman, asked Bob if he wanted to go to Lake Tahoe the following weekend. Bob agreed and told Bowman that I'd probably want to go along, too, which I did.

We arrived at Lake Tahoe about 7:00 p.m. on Friday. By 10:00 p.m., each of us had lost the $60 we'd brought with us to gamble. We looked at one another, and Bob asked, "Now that we're here and we're broke, what the hell are we going to do for the next two days?"

Bowman, who had a very charming southern accent, said, "Maybe I can do something." He left and came back an hour later with $300.

I asked, "Where did you get $300?"

"Mr. Harrah loaned it to me," he answered.

Then I asked, "Mr. Harrah? The owner of Harrah's Casino? Do you know Mr. Harrah?"

"No, but my daddy does," he responded.

I asked him, "So what does your daddy do?"

"He's the president of RJ Reynolds Tobacco Company."

Bowman's full name was Bowman Gray III. Years later while driving through northern North Carolina, I saw the Bowman Gray Highway, the Bowman Gray Memorial Hospital, and a number of other buildings named after Bowman Gray I and II. Bowman was an extremely charming, good-looking man, about six feet tall, and athletically built. He had blondish hair and a ready smile. He also started hanging around the house before David and I left, so I got to know him a bit and I liked him. He was always in a good mood and was great company.

Unfortunately, after loaning Bob and me $100 each, our luck didn't change, but we did make the money last the rest of the weekend.

☆ ☆ ☆

We were all told that the top thirty percent of our graduating class was guaranteed to go to Germany. There were sixty students in my class, and I ended up number fifteen. David was number one, which was no surprise. We all received our orders, and as it turned out, we were *all* sent to Germany. Once again, we were given two weeks' travel time to get to our departure point, which was Fort Dix, New Jersey. We were also given two weeks' leave, which meant that the Army had given me three monthlong vacations in just over a year. This was two months longer than Standard Oil gave my father, and he'd been with them for more than thirty years.

David invited me to drive with him to his home in Denver to meet his sister and his parents. I was thrilled and honored. He said that our first stop would be La Jolla, California, which I found out was a coastal community within the city limits of San Diego. We graduated on a Friday and had a party at the house, ostensibly because David, Doug, and I were leaving, but actually because it was Friday night.

Bob's Russian program lasted another five months. We joined the Army together and managed to stay together for a year. We hoped that he'd also be stationed in Germany, but we knew that Russian students went to Germany, Japan, and Alaska, so there was no guarantee.

David and I left about noon on Saturday for La Jolla. After about six hours, David said we were close. We drove into a beautiful downtown area, and judging by the spelling of the town's name, it looked to me like it should be pronounced "La Jah-la." Fortunately, I didn't say that out loud before figuring out that in Spanish, *La Jolla*, which means "the jewel," is actually pronounced "La Hoya." We strolled around and checked out the beautiful ocean vistas, which were truly spectacular.

We got in the car to head to our next stop, and about twenty-five minutes later, after driving south on the I-5 and crossing a bridge into the city of Coronado, David pulled up in front of the majestic Hotel del Coronado, which was featured in the 1959 movie, *Some Like It Hot*. I asked him how we were able to afford to stay there. He told me that the hotel was owned and managed by a friend of his family, and we were going to be his guests. We were assigned to a large room with two adjoining bedrooms and two baths. It was called a suite.

Our host requested that we meet him in the private dining room at 7:00 p.m. He also asked us to wear our uniforms. There were about twenty-five other people in the room, and many of the men had on tuxedos. Our host was an Italian man who was very dapper and gregarious. David and I sat on either side of him. He gave a delightful speech about David and his family, and graciously welcomed me as a friend of David's.

He advised us to make great use of our time in Europe. He said that American men were very knowledgeable about many things, but they were somewhat backward in other important areas. He smiled and said, "European women would be more than willing to teach two young American boys a great number of important things you could not learn at home or in school."

He looked at me at that point. I smiled to let him know that I knew what he was talking about. I hoped David didn't know what he was talking about because David, when he was completely sober, was somewhat of a prude. I didn't think he was religiously prudish, but rather, he had a sense of what he felt was proper and acceptable behavior. I noticed, however, that after a few drinks, his level of acceptable behavior came much closer to mine.

The meal was one more opportunity for me to discover foods that I'd never tasted before. I usually would never eat anything that I didn't recognize, unless it had peanut butter on it. But in the world that David lived in, I forced myself to eat things I'd never seen at home. I found out, much to my delight, that they were all very good.

The Army introduced me to the benefits of three meals a day. I recognized almost all of the Army food, except for fried okra, which I never tasted, because of the way it looked. However, David started me on a gastronomical adventure that went on for two years and was guided by a number of friends, all of whom were older and much more experienced than I was in the world of fine foods.

The next day, we started our journey to Denver. The most exciting part of the trip was driving through the Rockies, which I'd never seen before, except from a train or a plane. The trip was both exhilarating and educational. David was exceptionally well-educated and told me a number of things I never knew about the west. He presented a strong and persuasive argument for why Denver should be the capital of the United States.

The trip took us two days, and when we arrived, I was given a room in another very large and beautiful house that was owned by David's mother. His parents were divorced, and his father was the president of a large bank in Denver, as had been his grandfather before him. David's fraternal grandmother was the matriarch of the family and a leading member of Denver's high society. David's sister was an extremely attractive eighteen-year-old who'd just graduated from finishing school.

On the trip to Denver, when David wasn't talking about the glories of his home city and state, he reminded me that I'd pledged not to come anywhere near his sister, except to say hello or to engage in very innocent, pleasant conversation. I asked him what he was implying, and he said, "You know what I'm talking about."

I was offended and said, "David, you and I are friends. I would never disrespect you or your family."

He said, "I believe that, but you're also a soldier on leave, and you and I both know what soldiers do when they're on leave."

I was astonished and said, "You of all people know that as far as the Army is concerned, I am the furthest thing from a soldier. Second, I've told you that in my neighborhood, sisters and girlfriends of friends are forbidden territory."

David smiled. "I understand that, and I believe that, but I'm warning you. Don't go near my sister."

After I met his sister, I understood why he was so concerned. She was tall like David, and blonde like David, but so much more attractive.

His sister and I were introduced and started a polite conversation. After a few moments, she made a couple of snide comments about what she assumed was my background. I didn't get angry, nor was I really offended, but I figured I couldn't let those comments pass, so I gave her a quick evaluation of what I thought her weak points were. She was a little miffed and said, "You don't know me well enough to talk to me that way."

I looked at her and said, "My words, exactly."

She walked away.

The next day, David told me that we were all going to the opera in Silver City. He then, rather inexplicably, asked me if I had a tuxedo. I looked at him and said, "I don't think so. Maybe I left it in Carmel."

He said, "Well, you must wear a tuxedo, and I have a friend who's about your size. Let's go see him."

We drove a few blocks away from his stately house onto an even statelier driveway of an even statelier house. He introduced me to his friend, who was, indeed, about my size. We then went to his friend's bedroom and into his walk-in closet. He showed me about eight tuxedos and asked me which one I liked. I said, "You guys pick out what you think is appropriate."

I'd never worn a tuxedo, and I was surprised to find out that it was more than just a suit. I got shoes, socks, cufflinks, something they called studs, a black bowtie, a shirt without buttons—which is where the studs come in—suspenders, and a very wide, belt-like object they called a cummerbund. We then went back to David's house and got dressed.

We later drove to Silver City, which I think was about an hour's drive away. We first went into a restaurant that was next to the opera house. I sat next to David's grandmother, and David was on her other side. I said that I wasn't very hungry and managed to get away with just some soup and a BLT sandwich. Peanut butter and jelly weren't on the menu.

I knew that the opera was going to start at 8:30 p.m., and I became concerned when it was approaching 8:30 and nobody seemed to be moving. I leaned over to Grandmother Meyer and said, "I think the opera is about to start."

She smiled, leaned over to me, and said, "Young man, the opera will start when I get there," and it did.

It was actually an operetta with Rex Harrison, and in the chorus was a dancer who'd attended the same high school I had in Royal Oak, Michigan. She was a year younger than I was, and we didn't know each other. After the performance, we went to a private party at the restaurant and met the performers. I introduced myself to her and told her that I'd graduated from Royal Oak Dondero High School. She was very pleasant, said she knew of me, and was pleased to see me. She even gave me a kiss on both cheeks. I really think that she was being polite rather than truthful, but I was thrilled. I knew that David's sister was watching, and I thought she looked impressed. Even if my feelings were correct, I was honor-bound not to do anything untoward, but I still liked the idea that her interests were piqued.

The next night, there was a party at David's fiancée's home, which was a cattle ranch outside of Denver. David told me that his future father-in-law was in cattle and oil. By the size of the ranch, I figured he was in *many* herds of cattle and *hundreds* of tankers of oil. There were about 500 people at the party, and at one point, they were all in the living room. I had no idea how many rooms were in the house, but when I asked David where the bathroom was, he said that the nearest one was down the hall on the left. It was much larger than my living room at home. It had walnut wood paneling and a solid walnut door about ten feet tall. It was the most luxurious bathroom I'd ever seen, even in the movies.

At one point, David's sister approached me and said, "I need to talk to you, and I don't want my brother to know about it. If you go outside, there's another building about twenty yards away that's open. I'm going to leave now. You leave ten minutes from now and meet me there."

She then turned and walked away. I looked around, and David wasn't looking at us. He was on the other side of the room with his fiancée, which meant that there were about 498 people between him and me. I was sure he wouldn't notice me leaving. I knew I was taking a chance, and I also knew that I wouldn't do anything shameful, but I wanted to hear what she had to say.

I waited about ten minutes and then strolled outside. I reached the door of the other building just as David grabbed me from behind and put his arm around my neck.

He squeezed my neck harder and said, "I told you not to talk to my sister."

When he allowed me to breathe again, I told him, "We were just going to talk."

"And that's what I told you not to do," he said.

"I'm sorry, but I didn't realize you meant that quite so literally," I said.

"Now you do," he muttered as he escorted me back to the party. I never spoke to his sister again, except to say goodbye the next morning.

David and I corresponded while we were in Germany and talked about meeting someplace, but it never happened. After the Army, he went back to Denver and became a lawyer. I went back to Detroit, got married, had a baby boy, and started teaching. About four years after the Army, David and his fiancée got married. He sent me an invitation, but I couldn't afford to take the time off or spend the money. I answered his RSVP and sent them a small gift.

Twenty years later, I stopped in Denver to see another old Army buddy on my way home from a conference in Los Angeles. I called David to see how he was doing, and to ask if we could meet for a drink. He brought me up to date, but said he was in the middle of a big trial and couldn't get away. He did mention that his sister was very happily married.

☆ ☆ ☆

After the Language School, David and I met up at the Detroit International Airport at the end of our leaves. We planned to fly together to Fort Dix. On the way there, I asked him if he'd looked closely at our travel orders. He said he hadn't and asked me why. I said:

"Some clerk at the Language School promoted us to Specialist Fourth Class by mistake."

He looked at his orders and smiled. "You're right. You and I and five other German students from our class."

Normally, those who finished a six-month course weren't promoted, but those who graduated from the Language School after a nine month course were promoted to Specialist Fourth Class (Spec 4). This clerk had inadvertently made all of us Spec 4's on our travel orders.

I looked at David and said, "As PFCs [Private First Classes], we will be assigned duty every day until we're shipped out, but Spec 4's are non-commissioned officers and therefore don't have to do the shit details like KP and policing the area."

David looked at me and asked, "Are you suggesting we report in as Spec 4's?"

I smiled. "Why not? Nobody will know the difference, and you know we'll be at Fort Dix for probably two weeks, so why not enjoy ourselves? We can buy two pairs of Spec 4 insignias at the PX and just sew them on one fatigue shirt and one khaki shirt. When we get to Germany, we can take them off, and nobody will know the difference."

David said, "Count me in."

When we got to Fort Dix, we went to the PX before reporting in and promoted ourselves to Spec 4 on two of our shirts. A couple of the other guys from the Language School saw us. They predicted that we'd end up in the stockade, but they said they wouldn't give us away.

For two weeks, David and I spent our days and part of our evenings in the NCO club. We met a couple of WACs (Women's Army Corps) who worked in the office where the determination was made as to how troops were going to be transported to Germany. Most soldiers were sent to Germany out of Fort Dix by troop ships that took ten to twelve days to cross the Atlantic, and they were *not* luxury liners. The troops were stacked one on top of the other below deck, and the food was old K rations that were normally vomited all over the floor for the entire trip. I didn't know if all the stories were true, and assumed some of them had to be exaggerated, but I did know that I did *not* want to go to Germany seasick, if at all possible. I asked one of the WACs if she could help us get sent by Military Air Transport (MATS).

She smiled and said, "It depends."

"On what?" I asked.

She smiled coyly. "That's yet to be determined, but as soon as I decide, you'll be the first to know."

Apparently, we passed whatever test we had to, because David and I were among the few selected to fly, while most of our comrades went by ship. We flew from Fort Dix, New Jersey, to Newfoundland, and from there to Reykjavík, Iceland. From Iceland, we flew to Shannon Air Force Base in Ireland and on to Frankfurt, Germany. It was only the fifth or sixth time I'd flown, and military transports are two or three levels below coach. But David and I were confident that it was much more comfortable than the USS *Buckner*, and the trip was a hell of a lot shorter. On the flight over, David said, "That worked wonderfully, but I don't want to press my luck, so I'm going back to being a PFC."

I asked, "Why? We could have two weeks in Frankfurt pulling shit details as PFCs before they ship us out. Why not continue?"

He'd made up his mind. He told me that it was too risky, but I decided to push my luck. I even sent my mother a letter asking her to address any future letters to Spec 4, Gerard Teachman. Once again, no one questioned me. I didn't have to pull any details, and I had a chance to explore Frankfurt, which I knew could be a little dangerous because I was young and prone to being foolish.

I heard that we weren't allowed to go into an area of Frankfurt called Sachsenhausen, because it was known to be filled with Communists and Communist sympathizers. I was also told that there was to be a street carnival in Sachsenhausen, and there would be a lot of pretty young German girls. I was eager to try out my German, so I went to the Communist street carnival in full uniform.

I met some Germans, including two very attractive girls, and we ate bratwurst and drank apple wine.

I read a book in high school called *Arch of Triumph* by Erich Maria Remarque. In the book, which took place in Paris prior to World War II, everybody drank a form of apple brandy called Calvados. The book made Calvados sound so good and so romantic that I figured I'd try the German equivalent, which was what everyone else was drinking. I don't remember the taste being especially good or bad, but I do remember that the next day, I had the worst hangover I've ever experienced.

I also remembered exchanging hats with a German man who wanted my khaki Army hat that we used to refer to as a "cunt cap." I think the official name was garrison cap. He gave me his *müzen*, which was a round cap with a very small brim that students wore. That, in and of itself, was probably not dangerous, but on my hat was an insignia for the ASA.

After I emptied my body of every foreign fluid, and some that I believed belonged there, I thought about that incident. I decided that I'd gone way too far this time. Most of my relatives, including my brother, predicted that I'd ultimately end up in trouble and/or jail, and I think I was trying to prove them right. Fortunately, nobody mentioned that incident. I wasn't arrested, and we didn't go to war. In fact, the next day, we received our orders and shipped out to our duty stations. I was sent to Coburg, and David was sent to Berlin. They were both considered good stations.

The day before I shipped out, I was called into the captain's office. He looked at my orders and asked, "Teachman, are you a PFC, as your orders say, or a Spec 4, as the insignia on your arm says?"

I responded, "Sir, this is a matter of great concern to me. I graduated from the Language School with the same fluency in German that others had in a nine-month course in Russian. I felt it was only fair that I should become a Spec 4, if they were to become Spec 4's. When I got my orders to go from the Language School to Fort Dix and they said I was a Specialist 4th class, I figured the Army agreed with me and just forgot to tell me."

He looked at me without saying a word for quite a while. I tried to find any signs of kindness in his eyes. Eventually, he said, "You get those goddamn stripes off of your arms right now, PFC Teachman, and get your ass out of Frankfurt by tomorrow, at the latest. If you miss that bus, your ass is going to be in big trouble."

I was extremely grateful, but I knew that I should say as little as possible. I simply said, "Thank you, sir," saluted as smartly as I could, and left his office.

CHAPTER 4

My Introduction to Coburg, Germany

I arrived at Herzo Base, which is about ten miles from downtown Nuremberg, on a sunny but cool September day in 1958. There were two of us who were scheduled to report to the ASA field station in Coburg that weekend. Herzo base was a former German Air Force base situated on the outskirts of a town called Herzogenaurach, which is about twelve miles from downtown Nuremberg. It was the home base for four field stations located nearer the East German and Czechoslovakian borders.

The first time Don Van Stry and I met was the day after we arrived at Herzo Base. We and six other soldiers were assigned to a detail. We had to go down into the basement of one of the barracks, bring up all the storm windows, and load them onto a three-quarter-ton truck. As the sergeant led us downstairs, I saw one of the guys climb into the back of the truck. I came up with one large storm window and handed it to him. As he was stacking it, I jumped into the truck. He looked at me, smiled, and said his name was Don Van Stry.

I said, "I'm Gerry Teachman, and it seems as if we think alike."

The other guys brought up the rest of the storm windows, and Van Stry and I very carefully stored them in the truck. We did an excellent job, as did the guys who carried them up all those stairs.

Van Stry and I went to Coburg the next day with all of our gear in the back of another three-quarter-ton truck, or maybe it was the same truck we loaded the day before. The Army had an endless supply of three-quarter-ton trucks and jeeps. When we arrived in Coburg, they took us to what was called the *Kaserne*. That's the German word for "barracks," and these were the lodgings for the German border guard, or *Bundes Grenschutz*. Coburg was only about three miles from the East German border.

The Kaserne was a quadrangle of four buildings (four stories), three of which contained the German border guard. On the first two floors of the fourth building was a rotating unit from the 1st Calvary (Cav.), with its headquarters in Bamberg, Germany, which was about forty miles away. Every month, a new group from the 1st Cav. would rotate to Coburg. Their mission was to perform border surveillance and liaison with the German border guard. The ASA unit to which I was assigned was on the third floor of the 1st Cav. building. The building itself was called Harris Barracks, and the rest of the Kaserne, which was built prior to World War II, was called the *Hindenburg Kaserne*.

One of the buildings contained a German *Kantina*, or cafeteria, which was on the first floor. We could eat there (but we had to pay for it), or we could eat in the Army cafeteria, which was on the fourth floor of our building and served both the 1st Cav. and us.

The ASA is part of Army Intelligence, so we all had top secret crypto clearances. We were told not to fraternize with the German border guard or the soldiers from the 1st Cav. No one was to know what our mission was. We were thirty soldiers, all of whom spoke either Russian or German. Our operation's building was on top of the second highest hill for miles around, and it was dotted with antennas. Officially, we were a weather station, but most of the Germans and all of the 1st Cav. knew otherwise.

I was assigned a room, as well as a roommate named Tony Veccio. We each had a military bunk bed, a stand-alone closet for clothes, and a standard Army trunk at the end of our beds. Tony immediately set the rules:

- First, I wasn't to speak any German to him, because he'd been there a year already and he spoke fluent German, whereas I spoke "Monterey German." The implication was obvious.

- Second, Tony explained that I'd be working shifts. I'd start working the swing shift from four to midnight, then I'd work three days and have one day off, and then I'd start working the midnight shift for three days. It started at midnight and ended at 8:00 a.m. Then I'd have one day off. I would finish the cycle by working three days until 4:00 p.m., after which I'd have three days off.

Tony had a different job than I did, which required him to work the day shift only, but the same sequence of three on, one off, three on, one off, three on, three off. He didn't want to be bothered when I left to work the midnight shift, or when I returned from work on the swing shift. I was to be extremely quiet whenever I entered or left our room. I immediately figured Tony came from New York. I was close—he was from Philadelphia.

Tony asked me my age, and I told him I was twenty years old. He told me I looked younger, which, when you're that age, isn't a compliment, but it was something I was used to. He said he had a circle of friends, and he didn't need any new ones, especially a young friend. I'd already decided that Tony and I were never going to become close friends, so his rejection didn't bother me. He asked if I understood the rules, and I told him I did. He smiled and asked if I was hungry. I said I was, and then he said:

"Let me buy you your first German meal in Coburg."

He took me downstairs and out the door of our Kaserne. We crossed a well-manicured stretch of ground, which led to the front door of the Kaserne next to ours, over which was written in German script: *Kantina*.

It looked like all the pictures I'd seen of the inside of a German restaurant. The clientele were mostly Germans, most of whom were in the gray uniforms of the Bundes Grenschutz. It was set up cafeteria-style, and we got in line. The German in front of me spoke to the person he was with. It sounded to me like "Nah, da bin ie net." I asked Tony what language he was speaking. He said he was speaking Coburger Deutsch.

I asked him, "Really? What did he say?"

Tony clarified for me. "He said, 'Nein, das bin ich nicht.'"

He then explained that it meant: "No, that isn't me."

Rather than respond to his condescension, I just smiled and said thank you. Tony told me that each area of Germany had a local dialect, somewhat like our southern dialect, but more distinct. The local dialect is spoken at home and among family and friends. North Germans often say they can't understand the South German dialects, and vice versa. However, all Germans also speak

High German, which is understood throughout Germany. He said he could understand Coburger, but couldn't speak it and wasn't interested in learning it. After hearing one sentence of Coburger Deutsch, I decided I didn't want to learn to speak it, either.

After our snack of *würst* and *bröchen* (sausage and a roll) with "eine Coca Cola," I asked who the attractive woman was behind the counter. He said, "Her name is Anna-Liese, and you don't stand a chance. She's a refugee from East Germany and is not very fond of Americans."

After we finished our snack, which I loved, and Tony paid the bill (which was one mark, fifty pfennig). Tony said the exchange was 4.25 marks to $1. That meant 1.5 marks was less than fifty cents. We went back to the third floor of our building, and Tony led me to a large room down the hall called the dayroom. It had a ping-pong table, an old upright piano, a poker table, a couple of comfortable chairs, an old sofa, and about ten folding chairs.

This was during the day, so no one was playing cards or ping-pong. There were about five guys sitting in the room reading. Tony introduced me to each of them, but the two I remember best later became friends of mine. One was named Don Nelowet, and he was smoking a pipe. He looked up at me when Tony introduced me and said, "Just what we need—another fucking Joe College."

The other guys were much more congenial. One of them, named Pete Warner, was actually friendly.

Van Stry and I were driven up to work the next day, where we were assigned to teams, which the Army called "tricks," for a reason known only to the Army. A trick consisted of one sergeant or Spec 5 and six Spec 4's or PFCs. We worked together on all the shifts. Consequently, these are the guys that I'd get to know first.

Our "operations building" was at the top of the second-highest hill around Coburg, which is next to the highest hill. The top of our hill was flat, and I was told that it had been intentionally flattened by the Duke of Coburg during one of Germany's medieval wars. The flat surface prevented cannons from hitting Coburg Castle, which is on the top of the next hill. Coburg castle, in German, is called *Die Veste* (The Fortress), and it's the castle for the House of Saxe Coburg, whose most famous family member was Prince Albert, the consort of Queen Victoria. It is the only castle in Germany that was never successfully overtaken. The family home for the House of Saxe Coburg is at the bottom of the hill that the castle is on. It's called the *Ehrenburg Schloss*.

When Don and I jumped out of the back of the three-quarter-ton truck that delivered us to operations, there were two guys standing near the perimeter. We both noticed that they were laughing. They were looking at a dog that was caught in barbwire. We went over there to help these guys get the dog out, or so we thought. As the dog tried to make a move to loosen himself, these two guys would shake the barbwire and laugh. Neither Don nor I liked people who hurt animals, so we both rushed at these guys. As we got closer, we realized that both of them were bigger than we were, but we were committed. Don looked at the biggest guy and said:

"You now have thirty-two teeth. Would you like to try for none?"

The big guy stepped back and asked, "Who the hell are you?"

Don said, "That's not important; the important thing is that you are not to hurt this dog."

The two of them looked at us, shook their heads, continued laughing, and walked away. Don and I carefully eased the dog out from the barbwire. The dog immediately adopted us, and we him.

His name was Spunky, and he was one of six dogs who hung around our operations and were fed by us. This encounter was to end badly for all of us, especially Spunky, but not immediately.

At the Language School in Monterey, they never told us what our jobs would be after graduation. I was hoping it would involve interacting with female spies at cocktail parties, but I wasn't even close. I soon found out that what I was assigned to do was very boring. We each sat at a console that contained a radio receiver and a large tape recorder. We used the dial on the radio to search the frequencies that were used by the East German Army or the Russian Army.

As a German linguist, I was only interested in the East German Army's conversations, which were called "traffic." When I found something, I'd listen for a few moments, and if I could determine that it was actually communications within the German military, I'd turn on the tape recorder by foot pedal. That was all explained to me during my first day on the job. When I sat down at the console at the beginning of my first shift, I assumed that this was the beginning of eight straight hours of searching for German traffic.

I was the only new guy on the trick. They trained Van Stry with me, but he was assigned to another trick. Besides our trick, there were four other soldiers in the operations building—our first lieutenant was Tom Powers, and our first sergeant was Richard Brown, plus two soldiers who were called transcribers. They'd all been there since 8:00 a.m., and they all left around 5:00 p.m.

As soon as they were gone, one of the older trick members called down to a German restaurant for seven Wiener schnitzel sandwiches, which included one for me. Soon, one of the guys took the truck, picked up the sandwiches, and brought them back. There was a refrigerator in operations filled with soft drinks.

The operations building was a one story, wooden structure about sixty feet long, thirty feet wide, and fifteen feet high. It consisted of two small rooms for the two transcribers who listened to the tapes we produced, and would give them a very rough translation or transcription. The tapes were packaged up and sent to ASA headquarters in Heilbronn, Germany, on a regular basis by a courier. There was also an office in the front of operations where Sergeant Brown and Lieutenant Powers each had desks. The rest of this wooden building was one large room that had eight consoles lining one wall. The room also contained a large table, around which we sat when we had a meeting, ate, or played cards during the swing- and mid-shifts.

After we had our schnitzel sandwiches, which were absolutely delicious, I noticed that nobody went back to their consoles. Everyone stayed around the large table, and soon four of the guys were playing cards, including the trick chief, who was a Spec 5, and one other one was reading. Every once in a while, someone got up and went over to listen on one of the consoles for fifteen or twenty minutes. By 11:00 p.m., we started to straighten up everything to get ready for the trick change. The new trick would arrive about 11:45 p.m., and we'd go back in the truck they came in.

After three days of working this swing shift, we got twenty-four hours off. We didn't have to work until midnight on the following day. That night, the guys on my trick told me they were all going downtown, and invited me to come along. We went to a place off the town square (Marktplatz) to a restaurant called The Residenz Café. I was a little confused when I saw the sign, because the guys had been telling me that we were going to the Razi bar, and some said we were going to the Pit.

Once I walked inside, I could see why some of them referred to it as the Pit. It was a large room with the bar at one end that sat about fifteen people. There were about ten tables along the walls that surrounded a large dance floor. A small, six-piece band was opposite the bar, and everyone in the bar smoked, which produced a yellow cloud surrounding the ceiling lights. I expected to see Peter Lorre sitting at a corner table.

Most of the people in there were German, and many of them were women. It reminded me of a bar I'd gone to on the campus of Wayne State University the one year I attended before I joined the Army. It was called Anderson's Gardens, and it was a prostitute/hillbilly bar. It had a jukebox that played country music, and there were a number of good ol' boys who hung around. The college students were mostly single guys, and some college guys with college girls. Plus, there were some prostitutes.

The Pit didn't have a jukebox that played country music; instead, there was a small band that played traditional and contemporary Bavarian music. As far as I could tell, none of the Germans had gone to college. I don't believe any of the girls were prostitutes, but some appeared to be very friendly. The German men were working class and seemed to have two goals in mind: to get drunk… and to get drunker. A number of them had already accomplished both goals before we entered.

My friends took me to the bar and told me they were going to introduce me to a Coburg tradition. They ordered five shots of Escorial, which I'd never heard of. One of them counted one, two, three, and we each downed our shots. It was like what I assumed kerosene would taste like. One of the guys, Jack, then took his lighter and lit the fumes that were left in my glass. The blue flame burned for about twenty seconds.

I looked at Jack and asked, "How powerful is this shit?"

Jack said he thought it was about 140 proof.

"That's seventy percent alcohol. No wonder I could barely keep it down," I said.

Jack smiled. "The second one will be easier, and the third one you'll love."

I told him, "I'll have to take your word for that, because I'm not having a second one, and I don't believe I could live through three shots of that poison."

Jack gave me a stern look and replied, "You know, you have to go along to get along." He ordered two more for him and two for me. I knew I was going to get sick sooner or later, so I downed the other two shots. Jack lied. The third one was the last shot of Escorial I ever had.

Needless to say, the rest of that evening was a blur. I don't know how long I was at the Pit or what I did there. Also, I have no idea how I got back to the Kaserne, but I do know that I spent many painful hours in the latrine. The guys told me when they left that Jack was just getting started. I found out later that most of the people I knew handled Escorial about as well as I did. But for Jack, it became his drink of choice, which I found unbelievable.

☆ ☆ ☆

I soon found out that ours was not the only trick that did very little work during mid- and swing-shifts, and I started to question the value of what we were doing. The secrecy of the ASA was stressed from the moment I joined. The last day at Fort Devens, we were all marched to an assembly hall and heard a lecture from a colonel. He stressed the importance of our mission and ended his lecture by reminding us that no one was to know what our next assignment was. "For example," he said, "if your next assignment is Code School, you can't even tell your parents that. You must tell them that you're going to a specialized school at Fort Devens. That's it. No more."

I leaned over to Bob and said, "Our military address is U.S. Army Language School, Monterey, California. When I come home speaking German, I think my parents are going to put two and two together."

That was my first inkling that the Army was making a bigger deal out of our mission than was necessary. My second clue was when my mother sent me an article from our local paper announcing that Bob and I were being sent to Army Language School. How they got that information, I don't know, but I don't think it was from some Russian spy.

The final clue came about the eighth week I was in Coburg. We were working days when we were visited by a major, as well as a civilian who was from the National Security Agency (NSA). They were making a "support the troops" tour of the ASA outposts in Germany. The civilian gave a short speech and emphasized the importance of the mission. During his explanation, he told us what happened to the material we were gathering: "After you identify that what you're hearing is military traffic, and you tape it, those tapes and the transcriptions are sent to Heilbronn. If it's loud and clear, that is, five by five, or at least four by four, it is sent straight to Arlington Hall, Virginia, where it's read and evaluated."

Our trick chief said, "Sir, we never get anything that is that loud or that clear. The best we get is four by three. What happens to our traffic?"

The NSA official looked at Lt. Powers, who said, "It's because of the mountains between us and them."

"In that case, you're preparing for the day the big one comes down. At that point, all traffic will be essential," the NSA guy responded.

After the visitors and Lt. Powers left, someone said, "He just said we're practicing. Fuck that. I got this shit down. I don't need any more practice." He took off his earphones, walked over to the table, and started playing solitaire.

About two months after I arrived, the situation with Spunky the dog got ugly. The two guys Van Stry and I had stopped from torturing Spunky decided they were going to resume their perverted pastime. They enlisted a couple of other big game hunters to help. There were enough sane people there to have at least one good guy on each trick who would stop them. This didn't take much effort because, like all bullies, they were cowards, but it did make for a couple of tense situations.

One day while I was working days, Lt. Powers and Sgt. Brown came up to operations and said they were going to end this dispute by killing Spunky. I heard them say that to the trick chief. They asked where Spunky was as I walked over to the gun rack. We had a rack on the wall just inside the door of operations, in which there were seven loaded carbines. I picked up one of the rifles and walked toward the door. Lt. Powers saw me and said, "You don't have to kill him, Teachman. We'll do it."

"I'm not going to kill Spunky, and neither is anyone else," I said.

Nobody said a word for about twenty seconds, and then my trick chief walked over to me and asked me for the rifle. He looked into my eyes and could see I was scared. He looked over to Sgt. Brown and shook his head. Sgt. Brown walked over to Lt. Powers and said, "Let's talk this over," and they left.

"What the hell were you going to do?" asked my chief.

"I'm not sure, but I wasn't going to just let them kill Spunky," I said.

I didn't know it at the time, but Brown and Powers did talk it over and decided on another plan that they implemented about a month later. In the meantime, the bullies backed off.

Although Tony had made it very clear that he didn't need new friends, he eventually made an exception for me. He called me the "kid," as did a number of other people—partially because I was a couple years younger than most of them and also because I looked about sixteen years old. I didn't shave, my hair was brownish blonde, I was a little over 5'10", and I weighed about 160 pounds. Some people thought I looked German. Others thought I looked Scandinavian, but *everybody* thought I looked young.

Tony only had about five months to go before he was going home, and he was engaged to a very attractive German woman named Luzi. She was one year older than Tony, which made her about twenty-two years old, and she had a sister about two years younger who was named Kristal. Neither of them spoke English. Tony reluctantly admitted that my German was getting good enough so that when the four of us were together, we would all speak German.

Tony and I decided to rent an apartment in Coburg. It was relatively expensive, as far as the Germans were concerned, because it contained a private bath with a shower, kitchen, living room, and two bedrooms. I made about $130 a month, Tony made about $170, and the Army provided our room and board. That was the equivalent of what a German engineer was making. I don't recall how much Tony and I paid for the apartment, but between the two of us, it was affordable.

The first three-day pass I had, after we got the apartment, Tony invited Kristal and Luzi over for an Italian meal. He started cooking it the day before. I told him that I was a picky eater, but I liked Italian food. He said, "Franco American spaghetti is not Italian food."

"How about my mother's spaghetti?" I asked.

He said that didn't qualify, either. I was perturbed and asked, "How about my buddy Jerry Carcone's mother's spaghetti?"

"Where was she born?" he asked.

"Rome."

"I don't know. Maybe. But I'll guarantee you that my spaghetti is authentic Italian, and it's the best."

Tony made a huge batch of sauce the day before the party, and he put veal chops and chicken in it. He let it simmer all day, and we ate it the following day. The first course was spaghetti with just sauce. It was fantastic. Then we had rigatoni pasta with veal chops and an Italian salad. That was even better. Finally, we had penne pasta and chicken with the rest of the salad. Nobody could move. After about a half hour, Tony told the girls to clean up everything, which Tony said was an essential part of an authentic Italian meal.

After everything was cleaned up, Tony brought out what he said would have to pass for cannoli: light, creamy, German pastries that he served with espresso coffee. I was afraid to tell Tony that

I didn't like pastries, nor did I drink coffee, but I managed to get them both down.

It wasn't that I wanted to please Tony—I had another motive. Luzi and Kristal had brought a girlfriend to dinner, which indicated two things. Obviously, Kristal wasn't interested in me, and they thought I must be lonely. The girl's name was Monika, and she was from East Germany. She lived alone in her own apartment because her family was still in the East. She worked with Kristal in what would pass for a department store in Coburg. She was a window designer and had actually gone to school for window design. That was my first inkling that the German school system was somewhat different from ours.

We all told Tony that this was not only the best Italian meal we'd ever had, but probably the best meal *ever*, period. That didn't come as a surprise to Tony, who didn't lack confidence. Tony was about 5'9", with black wavy hair—not the Tony Curtis kind of curly hair that hung over the forehead, but rather the Robert Taylor kind that was combed straight back. He wore horn-rimmed glasses and wasn't what I would call handsome, but he was confident, interesting, and charming. He also had a touch of the bad boy vibe, which I was told, some women found intriguing.

I later learned that German women weren't that interested in handsome men, which I found encouraging. What they looked for instead was what they called good character, which included a good personality. They also said they liked a man with a body like actor Robert Wagner: not muscular and athletic, but slim and toned. And finally, they said they liked a man to have attractive hands that were well groomed.

Tony fit the bill, at least as far as Luzi was concerned—she was very much in love with him. I was somewhat surprised about that, because she was extremely beautiful and personable. I thought there was a number of better-looking and more attractive men around that Luzi would've found more appealing. But after other German women explained to me what they were looking for, I had a better understanding of why Luzi found Tony appealing.

I soon realized that I needed a car in order to take better advantage of my days off. The whole area around Coburg was filled with beautiful and historic sites. I asked my parents if I could borrow $400 to buy a car, and they lent it to me. I sent home $50 a month, but I usually asked them to send it back to me. My father insisted that I was asking for a gift rather than a loan, which turned out to be accurate, although I believed that it was my intent to pay them back.

Most of the guys I was stationed with bought three-year-old German cars, many of which were black Mercedes. The main reason was that the price of gasoline was very expensive in Germany... if you were German. American military personnel could buy gas coupons for thirteen cents a gallon, and all the European gas stations accepted the coupons. A three-year-old Volkswagen turned out to be almost as expensive as a three-year-old Mercedes, because those who could afford a Mercedes would get a new one every three years. However, if the average German looked for a used car, he wanted one that got the best gas mileage, which was the Volkswagen. Of course, this was only thirteen years after the war. Germans were still frugal, and the upper and middle classes were still relatively small.

My car was black, with a cloth roof that I could slide open. It had no gas gauge, but when it ran out of gas, I turned a switch, and it gave me another gallon. It also had a pump on the dashboard that I used to get grease to all of the joints. It had running boards and big headlights, and looked like every car I'd ever seen in old World

War II movies. The style of the Mercedes didn't change from the 1930s until well after the war.

When I got my next three-day pass, Tony suggested that we drive down to Garmisch, which was south of Munich. He was again willing to overlook his rule about new friends for two reasons: he didn't have a car, and being raised in Philly, he didn't know how to drive. The drive was about 160 miles from Coburg to Garmisch, which lay at the base of the tallest mountain in Germany. The mountain was not what attracted Tony, though; Garmisch had one of the best gambling casinos in Western Europe, and Tony was a gambler.

After we checked in to the hotel, we had dinner and then went to the casino. I'd been to Las Vegas and was used to their casinos, but this was more like something out of a James Bond movie. The croupiers and dealers were dressed in tuxedos, not polyester sport coats. There were no blackjack tables, which was the game I preferred. Here, people played roulette, baccarat, and poker. We went to the roulette table, and I was fascinated by the croupier, who took bets in three languages: German, English, and French.

Tony instructed me on the finer points of the game and suggested that I watch him before I played myself. I watched Tony play for about a half an hour, and he was down about $90. I went to another table and didn't play the game as Tony had instructed, but instead I bet my lucky numbers. After about an hour, Tony came to me and said, "This isn't my night. I think we should leave."

He looked at the pile of chips in front of me and asked, "Are those yours?"

I answered as humbly as I could. "Yes."

"How much did you start with?" he asked.

"Fifty dollars," I told him.

Tony looked at my chips again and said, "It looks like you have a lot more than fifty dollars."

I slowly counted my chips in front of Tony, and when the total hit $265, I looked up at him and smiled. "It must be beginner's luck." I cashed in and we left.

The next day, we decided to go up to the Zugspitze, which is the highest mountain in Germany. We took a small train most of the way up and then walked a short distance to the top. Tony wasn't in a good mood. He didn't like losing, and he hated me winning. On the way up, I saw a sign that said, "U.S. Army Personnel: Skiing." I looked at Tony and asked him if he'd ever skied. He shook his head no.

I said, "Me either. We should check it out on our way down."

He mumbled, "Okay."

It was a gorgeous forty-degree day, with bright sun and no wind. We got off at the end of the train and took a funicular up to the observation platform. There was a worn path leading from the observation platform to a higher elevation that looked like it might be a bit strenuous, but it was worth it. We hiked about fifteen minutes and arrived at the top of a peak with views that were breathtaking. I told myself that I was actually climbing an Alp, which was technically the truth, although I was dressed in a sport coat, slacks, and loafers. When we arrived at the top, I looked around and realized that everything was below me. I started to get vertigo.

I'd experienced vertigo only once before, and that was in Big Sur, California. David and I had eaten lunch at the cliffside Nepenthes restaurant and had walked around the area. I stepped to the edge to get a better view of the whole coast, when I realized that I was on somewhat of a ledge that was sticking out farther than the rest of the coastline. Suddenly I had this feeling that I wanted to jump. I didn't know what to do. I sank to my knees and crawled back about twenty feet. When I stood up again, the feeling of wanting to jump was gone. I thought:

What the hell is going on? I'm having the best time of my life. Why would I want to end it?

I talked to David about that later on in the day, and he said it was vertigo, which was a problem related to the brain. Having grown up in Colorado, he knew a number of people who'd experienced it. I was relieved that there was a name for what I'd felt. I didn't understand the relationship-to-the-brain part, but I knew that I didn't want to have that feeling again, and I didn't—until I got to the top of Zugspitze. Rather than fall to my knees again, I walked backward down the path for about twenty feet, so that I had something above me. There, I could look around and enjoy the vista without getting the feeling that I wanted to jump.

I didn't tell Tony about my experience, because I figured he'd use it against me. He already had enough ammunition. I knew that he was embarrassed that he'd lost money and that I'd won. He presented himself as a professional gambler from Philly, and I was just some young kid from Detroit. That I'd won and he'd lost just wasn't supposed to happen.

On the way back down the mountain, we checked out the skiing sign. We found out that skiing for the U.S. military was one dollar, which allowed us to get full equipment, including the ski parka, pants, boots, and a half-hour lesson. We put the ski outfit on over our civilian clothes, picked up the skis, and walked to the area where they gave lessons. Our lesson consisted primarily of how to put on the skis and how to stop, and some other things two smart guys like us didn't need to listen to. We put on our skis and waddled over toward the ski lift.

The instructor said that beginners should take the ski lift to its first stop, which was what he called the beginner's slope. If we wanted, we could go up higher to the intermediate slope. At the beginner's slope, there was a restaurant. Tony was never able to make it to the ski lift. He was either having a very bad run of luck, or he was one of the most uncoordinated individuals I'd ever seen. In either case, he concluded very quickly that he didn't like skiing and didn't want to try it. What he really wanted was a drink. I didn't think I was going to have many opportunities like this, and I inwardly gloated, since I could maneuver the skis and get to the ski lift. I told him that I was going to the intermediate hill and then I'd stop and meet him at the restaurant.

I took the ski lift past the beginner's hill up to the intermediate hill and started to ski, which to me meant pointing the skis downhill and staying upright. As I was going down that hill, it became quite apparent that I was going faster than most of the other skiers. And I didn't understand why they were zigzagging. I tried to remember if the instructor had mentioned that, but I didn't think so.

When I got to the restaurant at the beginner's hill, there was no way I was going to be able to stop. I waved briefly at the restaurant in case Tony was looking, and then I sped down the hill to the bottom. I saw people who were walking up toward the T-bar, and they were right in the path that was my ultimate destination. I had to make a decision. I knew at the speed I was traveling, I was likely to seriously injure them and myself. I called upon my Christian upbringing and decided to sacrifice myself instead of plowing into a large number of innocent skiers. I sat down and started tumbling down the hill. Ultimately, I ended up in a snowbank near the bottom. I was completely uninjured, except for my pride. I knew the saying, "God looks out for fools and drunks," and I decided that foolish beginner skiers were also included.

I turned in my skis and gear and walked up to the restaurant to meet Tony. He said he hadn't seen me go by and asked how it went. I said, "Fantastic." I confessed to him that I didn't know how to stop, so I took a small tumble at the end, but I left out the details.

The next day, we drove back to Coburg, and it was a fairly quiet drive. Tony's attitude toward me was different after that trip. I'd apparently gained some respect. In any case, Tony and I seemed to be friends, or at least better acquainted.

I spent my first Christmas in Germany in bed with the flu. It was my first Christmas away from home. The week between Christmas and New Year's was my favorite time of the year growing up in Detroit. I had a lot of friends and family, and we all got together and celebrated that whole week long. It seemed to me that everybody tried to be extra nice during that time. My mother spoiled me all year round, according to my brother, but even *I* agreed that she certainly did so during Christmas.

When I was about four years old, my mother took me to see Santa Claus at the largest department store in Detroit, which was called Hudson's. I asked for four toys and received three of them. I wasn't that disappointed, because the three toys I got were the three I wanted most. The next year, my mother took me again, and I asked Santa for four more things, and then said, "You better write these down, because last year, you forgot one of my presents."

He laughed and said, "It must have fallen off my sleigh, because Santa never forgets."

After my mother finished all of her shopping and we were leaving to go home, we walked past Santa again, and he yelled over to me, "Hey, little man, come tell Santa what you want for Christmas," thus making me, at five years old, a wiser, but less trusting soul.

Back in Coburg, I spent the entire week in a tiny room on an Army bunk bed, with no friends or family to share my Christmas with. It wasn't the first time in my life I'd felt sorry for myself—that had been one of my favorite activities in junior high school. It was, however, the first time I felt all alone.

About two weeks later, Lt. Powers announced whom he was sending to be a part of the Army's major winter exercises. These exercises were called maneuvers and took place twice a year. They were held in southwest Germany around a large Army base called Grafenwoehr. The exercises involved two armies, the Red and the Blue, who were to play war games against one another for a week. Lt. Powers sent a unit of ASA, which would be assigned to one of the armies for that week as a listening post. Lt. Powers picked six of us to go, and we were all friends of Spunky. Apparently, Brown and Powers had come up with a new plan.

The six of us drove a three-quarter-ton truck with all of our gear and a Jeep to Grafenwoehr. There, we were assigned a two-and-a-half-ton truck loaded with top secret communications equipment. A sergeant approached us upon our arrival and asked who could drive a "deuce and a half." No one volunteered, so he picked me. I told him I had more flying time in jets than driving time in huge trucks.

He smiled and said, "You look like a fast learner."

I said, "Okay, but I have two questions: Where are the keys, and how do you start this damn thing?"

The next morning, we loaded up and joined the Army convoy to drive to our designated stations. We were assigned to a company commander in one of the battalions, and they gave us a map published by Shell Oil Company with our destination marked in red pen.

An Army convoy consists of a very large number of vehicles, and we all drove on German highways along with German civilian cars. That first day, we drove for eight straight hours and covered ninety miles. The truck had six or seven gears—I've forgotten how many—but I never went fast enough to get out of third gear. We were told, even at that slow pace, that if we missed a cutoff, we had to go back about nine miles. I suggested to the guys that we were lost, and that wasn't a bad thing. I said we should go to the back of the convoy and find ourselves a nice, quiet place to spend the night. After a little hesitation, they all agreed. We decided to hook up with our designated company the next morning.

We drove at the back of the convoy for about thirty minutes before turning onto a side road that led to a wooded area. We circled the vehicles and put red warning signs around the communications truck that meant, "No Entering, Top Secret." We had loaded carbines and were told we were to "shoot to kill" any trespassers. We opened the K-rations we were given and found that the only thing edible was canned peaches.

Bavaria can be extremely cold in winter. We all had sleeping bags, which were comfortable, and most of the guys put them over their heads and were able to sleep. I could do that for about ten minutes, and then I'd get claustrophobic and have to come up for air. When my nose started to get numb, I'd cover my face again. It was a long night.

The next day, I suggested that we hang around the countryside for a few days before we report in. Bruce asked, "Wouldn't that make us AWOL?"

I said, "I don't think six GIs in uniform, driving around Bavaria in two trucks and a Jeep, would be considered AWOL. We'd be considered lost, which is what we are. We can find our unit eventually, just not today, or maybe not even tomorrow."

We drove around "lost" for four days. We spent each night in an area near a *gasthaus* (hotel/small inn). Three of us would sleep in the *gasthaus,* and the other three would stay with the trucks. We "found" our company the fifth day, and I was chosen to report in. I walked into the captain's headquarters, which was another two-and-a-half-ton truck made to look like an office, and reported to the captain. He looked at me and asked:

"Where the hell have you been, soldier?"

I said, "We've been looking for you, sir. You weren't where we were told you would be."

He said, "All that changed after our first-day fuck-up. Report back to Grafenwoehr tomorrow."

We read in the Army newspaper, *The Stars and Stripes,* that our exercise was the most successful one that the Army had had in ten years, despite the fact that four soldiers were killed when a tank ran over their tent while they were sleeping. I wondered how I'd react if my son were killed playing war games.

When we got back to Coburg, we wanted to know about Spunky. We took the Jeep and went to the Pit, knowing that some of our guys would be there. We were told that three of the guys had killed Spunky by beating him to death with a shovel. Sgt. Brown said that Sgt. Powers wanted it done while the six of us were gone. One of the guys was a

Spec 5 and a trick chief, which made him a little untouchable, but the other two guys were Spec 4's and weren't working that day.

We drove back to the kaserne, reported in, changed into our civilian clothes, and went looking for two of the killers. We divided into two groups of three, and our group went to the apartment that one of the guys rented. When he opened the door, we all walked in, and before he was able to say anything, Don decked him, and he went down.

One of us, maybe me, yelled, "Get up!"

He rolled into a fetal position and just stayed there. Bruce kicked him a couple of times, but I couldn't do it.

I said, "Why, Pat? And why with a shovel?"

He said, "We were ordered to do it. Jack and I got drunk first, and Jim suggested the shovel. We were told not to use a gun."

When we left, Pat was still on the floor rubbing his jaw and crying. We were also told by Dave that after being slapped around, Jim didn't fight back, either.

All three of Spunky's killers were short-timers and left Coburg within the next month to be transferred back to the States and discharged. I don't know how their lives turned out, but I hope they became better people.

About two weeks into February, I received a letter from my friend Bob McCall. He was in Germany, had spent a wonderful two weeks in Frankfurt, and was now in Heilbronn. Heilbronn was the ASA headquarters for Germany, and Bob was miserable there. He had no money and couldn't travel, and wondered if I could come and see him. He said he was in dire need of a friendly face and a loan. As it happened, Tony had a friend in Heilbronn that he wanted to see, so the two of us took a three-day pass.

It was great to see Bob and to catch up on all the people we'd known in Carmel. Tony had a very good time with his friend. We went our separate ways for the two days and were going to leave the morning of the third day. This would've given me ample time to drive back and report to work at 4:00 that afternoon for the swing shift. Unfortunately, Tony woke up feeling very sick.

I asked if Tony was really sick or just hungover. He said it was probably a combination of both. He told me that he had diarrhea and constantly felt like he was going to throw up. He said he didn't want to make that long car trip back to Coburg and suggested that we go back the next day. I reminded him I had to be at work at 4:00 p.m. He said this happened all the time and that he'd call and get somebody to work for me. He reassured me that everything would be fine. He didn't tell me whom he called, but I assumed it was the guy we called "Big Frank." He and Tony were very close friends, and they both were transcribers and Spec 5's.

Tony stayed in bed that whole day, so I had another day to talk with Bob. He now had some money, and I had a little less. We went to dinner and planned our next trip together. We decided that we'd go to Barcelona, Spain, whenever he was settled and had accumulated enough money and leave time. We both ordered "Wiener schnitzel mit pomme frites." It came with a small salad. As Bob started to eat his, I asked him if he'd ever heard of a honey wagon, and he said he hadn't.

"They should have given you this lecture when you arrived in Germany," I told him.

Then I explained to him that the Germans gathered human waste, which they put into a large, round barrel that they carried on the back of a cart called a honey wagon that was pulled by either a small tractor or a horse. They would drag that over their fields, and it would nourish the vegetables. I told him that it would also impart what was in their human waste, and that could be quite different from what our bodies were used to.

"Therefore," I warned, "we're not supposed to eat their fresh vegetables. If they're cooked, everything's fine, but stay away from salads." Bob pushed his salad aside and turned a pale shade of green. He did enjoy his Wiener schnitzel and French fries, though. At the end of the meal, he ordered a dessert, and I told him I didn't want any. I then started to eat my salad and his. He looked at me and blanched. Then we both started laughing, and he ate the rest of his dessert, but with a little trepidation.

Tony felt much better the next day. After breakfast, we drove back to Coburg. As we walked into the third floor of our barracks, we were greeted by Sgt. Brown. He looked at Tony and me and said, "You guys were supposed to be back yesterday. You've been reported AWOL."

Tony started to laugh. "You must be kidding. We both arranged to have our jobs covered."

Sgt. Brown said, "That's true, but that does not excuse your absence."

Tony looked at him. "I've done this before and have never needed to get an excuse from you or from Lt. Powers."

Sgt. Brown said, "I don't remember that, and this time the situation is a little different. Pack up your gear and report to Herzo Base tomorrow morning."

I could see Lt. Powers in the background, and he had a shit-eating grin on his face. I was the new guy, and I didn't say anything, but I had a feeling that this involved me more than it involved Tony.

The next day, Tony and I drove down to Herzo in my car and

reported in to the company commander. He read us a citation declaring that we were charged with two offenses. The first charge was, "Failure to report," and the second was, "Absent, without leave." He gave us a copy of the Uniform Code of Military Justice and said that he'd give us two days to review the book and would send over an attorney who would discuss our options.

Herzo Base was run by strict Army rules, and it was known to be a chickenshit base. All the soldiers in Germany were supposed to obey the military curfew—basically, we had to be back at the post by midnight. It also stipulated that all American soldiers had to wear ties after 6:00 p.m. This meant that the overwhelming majority of American soldiers had to buy civilian ties because their entire civilian wardrobes consisted of blue jeans and plaid shirts.

In the evening, you'd see the soldiers leaving their bases heading toward town in jeans, plaid shirts, and neckties. They couldn't have been more conspicuous if they'd been wearing signs or ringing bells warning the German populace, "Beware, the GIs are coming."

When the Army attorney, who was a captain, interviewed Tony and me, he asked us what we were going to plead. He was surprised to hear me say that I was going to plead not guilty. He asked if I was absent without leave, and if I'd failed to sign in. I told him that part was true, but I also told him the whole story, emphasizing Tony's illness and that I believed what we did was common practice.

"If that were true," he said, "then why did Lt. Powers press charges?"

I said I didn't know for sure, but I believed that Powers had something against me personally. I told him that I'd been seated with three English-speaking German friends in a *gasthaus* in Coburg when Lt. Powers came by our table. He told me that he was disappointed with my work output.

He'd said, "Teachman, I copied more traffic today than you have in the last two weeks. You better step up."

The captain looked at me and asked, "Do you really intend on bringing in three German nationals to testify on your behalf?"

I replied, "Yes, I do. I didn't do anything that I thought was wrong. Tony and others told me that this was common practice. Tony was sick and couldn't make that drive comfortably. I felt that as long as my workstation was covered, and it was, I was fulfilling my duties. I think Lt. Powers is prejudiced against me, because he found out that I'd slept with a girl he thinks is his girlfriend. I don't know how he found that out, but I think she may have told him. I wasn't aware at the time that Lt. Powers thought she was his girlfriend. When I found that out, I never went out with her again."

"Why not?" he asked. "You and Powers aren't friends, are you?"

I said, "No, but where I come from, you don't mess with someone else's girlfriend."

I told him that I'd also found out that there were a number of guys in our company who were sleeping with this woman. She wasn't very loyal or very choosy. I felt kind of sorry for Powers. A lot of guys were laughing behind his back, and I figured he knew it. Maybe he believed that he could take a stand against me because I was new.

The captain asked Tony, "What about you?"

Tony said, "I don't think he has anything against me, but I'm scheduled to go home soon, anyway."

Tony went on to tell him about the conflict over Spunky. He said that Lt. Powers knew that he and I were part of the group of soldiers who were protecting the dog.

Tony said, "I believe Powers is trying to get rid of the whole group."

We didn't hear from the captain for three days. When he came back, he said that we were going to be charged with a summary court martial. I told him, as I understood the Universal Code of Military Justice, that we'd be allowed to have an attorney for a summary court martial. He said that was correct. I asked when we could see him, and he said within the next two days.

When we met with the attorney, he had one question: "Do the German witnesses speak English?"

I told them all three spoke English very well.

The next day, which happened to be my twenty-first birthday, the captain came to Tony and me and said that there would not be a court martial of any type.

We asked him why, and he said, "I don't have to tell you why, but I will. What you're accusing Lt. Powers of is a serious security breach. The camp commander is returning to the United States in two months, and he doesn't want any court martial that may involve a security breach, because a security breach leads to an investigation into both the officer and his commanding officers. That could lead to a long trial. Consequently, your court martial is in the bottom drawer of the camp commander's desk. And it will stay there."

He continued, "Lt. Powers is being denied his promotion, and he's being given a reprimand for conduct unbecoming an officer."

He then went on to say they felt from the beginning that Powers was overly eager to punish us because he charged us with two counts, one of which was failure to report, and also being absent without leave. Lt. Powers, in their mind, was not only prejudiced against one or both of us, but he was also clumsy. If we'd pushed for a summary court martial, our attorney would have used both of those issues.

I asked, "Does that mean we're going back to Coburg?"

He said, "I don't think that would be a good idea, at least as long as Lt. Powers is still there. After he leaves, you can apply to go back, if they need you."

Tony and I were thrilled and delighted. We both wished we could have been there when Powers got the news. I made a vow to myself that I would get back to Coburg. There was no way I wanted to spend the rest of my time in the Army wearing a tie after dark.

Tony wasn't as upset as I was. He was scheduled to go back to the United States in about eighteen days. His major concern was his girlfriend, Luzi. The next opportunity he had for a three-day pass, he went up to Coburg and spent that time with her, saying good-bye. I went with him, because I had the car. I also spent time with him and Luzi, and was absolutely convinced that Tony was sincere. I believed he was madly in love with Luzi, and I could understand why. She was a lovely person in more ways than I could count. After they made their tearful farewells, we drove back to Herzo in silence.

Tony was a Spec 5, and because he had only two weeks left, he wasn't given any assignments. I was assigned to a work duty that had nothing to do with my German language training. I still worked shifts, but I was assigned to a giant building that was an old German airplane hangar. It was filled with tape recorders and radios. Each man sat in front of his station, either listening to overseas phone calls or five-digit code messages from secret agents.

The secret agents would contact us on a scheduled basis that was arranged with the agent's handler. We received the schedules for these calls each shift. The messages were in five-digit code in Russian, so I was taught how to count to nine in that language. I was told they changed the code each day, which made it virtually impossible to break them.

Every once in a while, we got a notice that a particular agent wasn't reporting on schedule. We were to try again for three straight days. If we received no response, we were to assume that the agent had been discovered.

A short time after, I was transferred to radio phone calls intercept. I was surprised and a little shocked to find out we were eavesdropping and recording shortwave radio conversations made between friendly countries such as Germany, France, England, and Italy. I thought that was against the rules. We also listened to radio phone conversations from Russia to other countries.

At that particular time, international and transnational phone conversations were all done through radio waves. An operator was contacted to call someone in another country, and then call back the individual who placed the call. They would do that by establishing a particular time that the two parties would call back. If someone in Germany wanted to talk to someone in the United States, given the six-hour time difference, this could become complicated. I never found out how we knew, but each shift, we'd be told to go to a certain frequency at a particular time and monitor the phone call. All of the operators in all of the countries spoke English, except for the calls between Russia and China, when both operators spoke Russian.

Some of these operators got to know one another. I remembered one female operator from Cairo and her contact in Moscow, who was a man. As soon as the two made contact, the Russian man would say, "I love you," to the Egyptian woman, usually in more than one language. She would giggle, tell him that he was being silly, and that he had to get back to work. But he would continue to profess his love and admiration to her, as well as his fantasies *about* her. One time, they arranged to meet in Cairo. After that, I never heard them talking to one another again. Perhaps they'd been found out, or maybe they ran off and emigrated to Detroit, got married, had children, and lived happily ever after. I'd like to think so.

There were even phone calls between people in New York and Europe that were monitored and recorded. Most of these calls were business related. I thought that if a person were unscrupulous and knew something about the stock market, he could probably make some money. Some of the conversations were funny, and we put those on the loudspeakers so everyone could listen.

As I mentioned earlier, I wasn't in the habit of working full eight-hour swings and midnight shifts in Coburg; however, with 200 men working and a bunch of officers supervising, it was very difficult to sleep on the job at Herzo Base. It was even more difficult for me to stay awake, especially during the midnight shift. I wasn't willing to sleep in the evenings before starting my shift. I would report on time at midnight and go right to work. When I had a ten- or fifteen-minute break, I would go into the latrine, sit on the toilet, and fall asleep for ten minutes. The Army taught me how to take ten-minute naps, but I had to be careful that I didn't do that too often. I didn't want to get caught and get into further trouble. My goal was to get back to Coburg, and I didn't want to do anything to jeopardize that.

I can remember as vividly as if it were yesterday that one evening, I left operations after a tedious midnight shift and walked to the mess hall. I slowly ate my breakfast and then walked directly into my barracks. I carefully pulled back the sheets of my bunk and slipped into bed, and said to myself, "I will always appreciate the luxury of being able to go to sleep when I'm tired." To this day, I still appreciate that luxury.

I also told my comrades that if we were ever overrun by the enemy, they wouldn't have to torture me. Just keep me awake for twenty-four hours and I'd tell them everything I knew, and if that wasn't enough, I'd make something up.

Three days before Tony left for the States, he handed me twelve letters he'd written to Luzi. He told me he'd written her one letter every day, from the time we left Herzo. He wanted her to receive a letter a day while he was returning to the United States via a troop ship. He asked me to mail one on the first day after he shipped out, and then mail the rest on each consecutive day. I promised him I would do that. And I sat with him while he cried and told me how much he loved Luzi, and how anxious he was to get her to the United States.

At that particular time, if a GI wanted to marry a German, he had to apply for permission, and have that application approved. That process sometimes took two or three months. A number of soldiers told German women that they would make that application when they got home and had resettled. Too often, that didn't happen. Among us, that became known as "pulling a GI."

I would have bet a lot of money that Tony would never pull a GI. I was wrong. The last letter I sent to Luzi was the last letter she ever received from Tony. I would go to Coburg to see her as often as I could, to ensure her there had been some mistake. I was convinced that Tony loved her and wanted to marry her, but after three months of no contact, even *I* had to admit that Tony had pulled a GI.

Before I got out of the Army, one of our friends went to Philadelphia after his discharge and looked up Tony. He asked him what had happened. Tony just shrugged his shoulders and said, "I wasn't good enough for her."

My friend told me that Tony looked terrible, drank too much, and worked as a bookie. Apparently, Tony was right.

Luzi and I remained friends, and she eventually married a German. They lived in Schweinfurt, which isn't far from Coburg, and when I left Germany to go back home, I stopped by and saw her. I was hoping everything had worked out well for her. She deserved the best. She was one of the finest people I'd met in Germany. We went out to lunch, and she told me that she was extremely unhappy and depressed. I tried as best I could to comfort her, but when I left, we were both crying.

There were about twelve guys that I worked with who stayed in the same barracks and worked the same shifts. I got to know them fairly well, and they were an interesting group. One of the guys, Dick Pantano, was from New York, and he reminded me of Holden Caulfield, the protagonist in *Catcher in the Rye*. He was about 5'7" and was extremely outgoing. I soon found out that he was also very funny, and one of the best people watchers I've ever known. We went into Nuremberg together very shortly after I started working with him, and we were sitting in a café, where we met two German girls. After a moment, one of the girls excused herself and went to the lavatory. The other stayed at the table with Dick and me. He leaned over and whispered in my ear, "Apparently, German girls can piss by themselves."

Dick was two years older than I was and had gone to a private boy's school in New York. His mother had left his father when Dick was ten and his younger brother was six. Their father worked for *The New York Times* as a typesetter, and wanted the boys to have a good Catholic prep-school education.

After Dick and I became good friends, he felt comfortable

enough to start correcting my English. He asked if I was sure I'd had one year of college.

I assume I started speaking a Detroit dialect of English during my hoodlum wannabe stage, at age thirteen. I wasn't aware of it, because I spoke like my friends did, but my parents often corrected me. That did no good, because I wasn't worried about being liked by my parents. I felt that was part of their job description. I was, however, worried about being liked by my friends and knew that their acceptance of me was always tenuous.

I graduated from high school with a B average and successfully completed one year of college. Dick asked me why I said things like:

"'Him and me are going to the show;"

"I seen him yesterday;" and

"Just between he and I."

I started to become self-conscious. I soon realized that my vocabulary was probably limited to that of a tenth-grade C student, compared to Dick's. He had a slight New York accent, but his grammar was correct, and his choice of words both baffled and fascinated me. I remember one day that he said he couldn't finish a book he was reading because it was too soporific. I asked him what that meant, and he told me that *soporific* meant "boring to the point of sleep." I found that word very useful when I went to hear any lecture given by Army officers, and after the Army, it fit far too many lectures I heard at the university. He also taught me the meaning of *solipsistic* (being extremely egocentric), which is another useful word that describes many people I've met.

I told all of my new friends at Herzo that my goal was to go back to Coburg. After laughing hysterically, they all told me that my chances were absolutely nil. They said that everyone at Herzo wanted out of Herzo, and I'd had my chance, but that I'd messed it up. I said that was probably true, but I was still going to try. What I had going for me was the fact that I was trained as a German linguist, and I wasn't using that training at Herzo. The same was true for Dick. He was also a German linguist, but the rest of the guys, although they were in the ASA, were trained in other areas.

I was anything but enthusiastic about my job at Herzo, and I let everybody know it. I was also somewhat outspoken about my feelings toward the chickenshit rules that one had to follow at Herzo, especially the wearing of a tie after 6:00 p.m. and having to be back before midnight, which only applied to Army personnel. The other services were exempt.

I also took as many three-day passes as I could. We were normally allowed only one three-day pass per month, but I'd get the first pass each month that I was entitled to, then make up some type of story to get a second pass. I don't remember all the stories, but the one my sergeant liked most was that I'd impregnated a German girl who notified me that she didn't know what to do. I needed to go see her, and help her.

The sergeant was a firm believer in maintaining good relationships with the Germans. He started to doubt my story when I used it the second time, and the third time, he said no. I told him that if he didn't give me the pass, I was going to ask the captain, because I was very upset and wanted to assume my full responsibilities as an American soldier. The sergeant and I were having a duel, and he had a shotgun and I had a peashooter, but I won sometimes, which truly bothered him.

His greatest victory was denying me what could have been the vacation of a lifetime. David sent me a letter from Berlin saying that his sister was having her coming-out in Versailles, France. She wanted David and me to be her escorts, and his family was inviting me to spend a week in Paris and the Loire Valley. All I had to do was bring my Army dress uniform. I naturally accepted, and was so excited about this new adventure that I actually had one of the guys teach me how to do the Emperor's Waltz, which I understood was one of the things I'd have to do with David's sister. I was then, and still remain, a very bad dancer, so it wasn't an easy task. My buddy finally said that my dancing was passable.

Two weeks before my leave began, my sergeant came to me and said that my leave was canceled.

I looked at him in shock and said, "What? My leave was approved a month ago!"

He said, "Yes, but it's been canceled, because one of the other guys has to leave during that period, and we can't have two guys from our squad missing at the same time."

I asked who the other guy was.

He smiled and said, "Me." He walked out the door laughing.

Although my father had drilled into me the idea that I should be as honest as possible at all times, as his second commandment he'd also taught me his first: "Thou shalt never intentionally commit pain." I tried to follow those two commandments. My father wasn't religious; in fact, he was an agnostic, but his two commandments made a great deal of sense to me. I knew that I was often dishonest with the Army, but my father had never been in the Army. I hoped he would understand that I was just learning how to play their game, at least well enough to win a few times.

☆ ☆ ☆

About a week after my sergeant canceled my leave, a number of guys I knew received their Spec 4 stripes. The Army issued most of its promotions on the basis of what they call "time in grade," which meant that after being one rank for a specific period of time, you'd be eligible for a promotion to the next rank. The guys who were promoted had the same amount of time in grade as I did, but my name wasn't on the list.

I went to the sergeant and asked him why. He started laughing. I had more than an inkling that this was going to happen, so I'd studied the Universal Code. I found out that if someone with sufficient time in grade was passed up, he could request a transfer, unless there was a written explanation as to why the promotion was denied.

The sergeant told me that I'd get the written explanation, but I never did. Instead, I got promoted. The rumor was that the sergeant went to the lieutenant and asked him to write the explanation. The lieutenant declined, so he asked the captain, who also declined. Apparently, the sergeant didn't like putting his anger on paper, so I became Spec 4, Gerard W. Teachman, which included a pay raise of about $50 a month. That was about a thirty-five percent raise, and with a dollar being worth 4.25 marks, it gave me much more buying power. It was also a small victory over my sergeant.

Around the beginning of June, I heard that Lt. Powers was rotating back to the United States. I went to the company commander, who was a captain, and asked him if I could be sent back to Coburg. He knew the story of my court martial and what had happened. I told him that my friends in Coburg told me they needed one more German linguist. He said, "Well, that might be true, but aren't you also needed here?"

I told him, "No, I don't think so, sir."

He asked me how I could prove that, and I suggested he call my sergeant. He could tell him he needed someone to work temporarily in the motor pool and ask if there was someone he didn't need who could do that. The captain smiled, picked up the phone and called the sergeant, who said, "I can give you Teachman for as long as you want him."

The captain put the phone down, looked at me, and said, "I don't know how you did this, and I don't want to know, but I'll send you back to Coburg next Monday. Lt. Powers is to report here this Friday."

Before I had my shift, I went down to the barracks where Dick and the rest of the guys were. I told them that I was going back to Coburg, thinking they'd be happy for me. I was almost 100 percent wrong. Dick was happy for me and congratulated me, and even told me that he'd miss me. The other guys were openly angry and wanted to know how I did it. A couple even went so far as to tell me that I was the biggest slacker in the group, and for me to be rewarded wasn't fair. I decided not to tell them how I did it, because I was afraid they might sabotage me. I left it up to them to figure it out.

CHAPTER 5

Back to Coburg

When I got to Coburg, I found out that they needed two German linguists. I suggested to the new officer that Dick was in Herzo and not doing any German. He sent for Dick, and we were able to continue our friendship while both of us were in the Army and also out of the Army. We remained good friends until he passed away a few years ago from stomach cancer.

A week after I returned to Coburg, I was told to go back to Herzo and report to the captain. I had no idea why, but I suspected it had something to do with Lt. Powers. When I walked into the captain's office, Lt. Powers stood there with that same shit-eating grin on his face.

The captain said, "Lt. Powers received a report that you were observed speeding through a German village last weekend. Were you?"

"A report from whom? The police?" I asked.

Powers said, "No, it was a private citizen."

"How do you know it was me?"

"He took down your plate number," the captain said.

"You're saying that a private citizen, with pencil and paper handy, saw a car speeding through his village with American military plates and saw well enough to copy the exact plate number. Are you sure he didn't make a mistake? What day and what time was this supposed to have happened?"

"I don't have that information," he said. "All I have is your plate number, and that's good enough for me."

I looked at the captain and asked, "Does this sound reasonable to you?"

The captain turned and walked out the door, saying, "This is between you and Lt. Powers."

He also looked at Lt. Powers and said, "The maximum penalty is a two weeks' suspended license."

After he was gone, Lt. Powers said, "Hand over your license."

I took out my wallet, handed him my license, and asked, "Aren't you rotating back to the States next week?"

He smiled and said he was.

"How do I get my license back?"

"I'll send it to you," he said as he tore it into little pieces and walked out the door.

Two weeks later, I asked Sgt. Brown if he had Lt. Powers' new address. He laughed and said, "Yes, I do. Are you going to send him a thank you note for taking away your license?"

"Yes, he tore up my military license, but I still have my civilian license." I showed it to him. "I think I'm now ineligible to drive any military vehicles."

☆ ☆ ☆

Don Nelowet had brownish-blondish wavy hair, which he parted on the left. His eyes were blue-gray. He had high cheekbones and a prominent nose, plus a rather thick lower lip. He wasn't what I would call handsome, but there was something about him that women found extremely attractive. They told me they liked his voice, which was somewhat nasal, but registered in the lower tones. What I liked about him was his confidence. I had no idea where he got it, and I wasn't quite sure if he'd earned it, but it was real.

I first met Don back on that first day in Coburg. He'd referred to me as "another fucking Joe College." But it wasn't long before he and I had opportunities to get to know one another better. That usually happened when guys worked with somebody on the same swing or midnight shift. Don, like Tony, was a transcriber and only worked during the day. He spent a lot of his off time in the dayroom, and like many of us, he went to the movies almost every night.

The Army had an interesting definition of deprivation. They assumed that because thirty of us lived in a German barracks without any PX or other trappings that came with Army bases, we were deprived. Consequently, they gave us two perks we wouldn't normally have: we were sent a new film every other day, which played in a little theater in our barracks; and we were given the privilege of buying alcohol in the Class VI store in Bamberg. This perk was normally limited to married personnel who were sergeants or above.

I could buy four large bottles of scotch whiskey a month. Chivas Regal cost me $4, and Dewars was $3. I was told that I could sell them both on the black market for about $50 a bottle, but it was illegal. I didn't want to leave Coburg, so I never tried to sell it. I usually served scotch at parties and/or gave bottles away as gifts. Germans liked whiskey, but their favorite alcohol was either

Schnapps or cognac. In fact, my drink of choice in a bar was a German cognac called Asbach Uralt, and Coca-Cola. It tasted like a rum and Coke and went down easy. It had the added advantage of being so sweet that I couldn't drink more than two or three at a time, and it was very affordable.

One of the guys was in the habit of ordering his cognac by the half bottle for himself and his guests. He was from Oklahoma and introduced me to two songs I still remember: "Long Black Vail," and "Rebel Soldier." He was a nice guy when sober, but I learned the hard way to leave the bar after he'd ordered his second half bottle. When he consumed enough fire water, he would stand on a table and proclaim to the world that he wanted to "fuck, fight, or ride wild horses."

He seldom got laid, and Coburg was out of wild horses, so he spent a lot of time fighting. Like a lot of good ol' boys I met, it made no difference whom he fought, why he fought, or if he won. I made the mistake of staying too long a couple of times and found myself wrestling with him on the dirty, beer-soaked floor of Big Mamoo's bar. I subdued him both times, before either of us got badly hurt, but he'd look up at me and say, "You know, Teachman, you're going to have to whoop me again next time."

☆ ☆ ☆

I took great advantage of both of our deprivation perks. I went to see whatever film was playing whenever I could. The films were only shown once a night, starting at 7:00 p.m. There was a group of us who were constant moviegoers. After the film, we either went to a restaurant or to the dayroom to discuss the film.

Don always had an interesting take on the movies. I agreed with him most of the time, and learned from him almost all of the time. When he was at the Army Language School, he acted at the Wharf Theater in Monterey. This interest in acting and theater was something I shared, but never had the courage to do. He was also interested in philosophy, and that was something I also wanted to study. Philosophy became the basis of many of our conversations, and eventually the foundation of our friendship.

The other thing we had in common was our interest in women. He didn't have a steady girlfriend when I met him, and I did. That January, I was introduced to the German season of celebration following their New Year, called *Fasching*. It's the equivalent of Carnival and Mardi Gras in New Orleans, but it lasts much longer and is very popular in southern and central Germany. In January, there were Fasching parties every Friday and Saturday evening. The closer it got to Ash Wednesday, which is the first day of Lent, the more frequent the parties became. Sometimes there were Fasching parties on Wednesday, Friday, Saturday, and Sunday evenings. The final weekend, as well as the Monday and Tuesday before Ash Wednesday, is when Carnival is celebrated in most Catholic countries.

Many of these parties were advertised in the newspapers, and frequently were costume parties around a theme. On one three-day pass in Munich, a friend and I saw an ad for a bikini Fasching party at a well-known nightclub. We decided to go, but we first had to buy a European men's bikini, which was like a silky jockstrap. We donned our costumes under our dress clothes and entered the building.

It took us both a couple of drinks before we could disrobe and join everyone else. There must have been 200 people, ages sixteen to sixty, in bikinis, dancing all night, taking turns with whoever was nearby. I've never seen anything like that since. There was one scene in the movie *Caligula* that came close, though.

One night, I talked Don into going to a Fasching party with my girlfriend and me. She decided that Don should go dressed as the devil. She had a girlfriend who sold makeup in the department store where she worked, and she fixed her girlfriend up with Don. We all met at the girlfriend's apartment. She had a costume ready for Don that consisted of a red cape to go with a red shirt and black pants that he owned. Then she made up his face to look like the devil, with dark, sunken eyes and red facial color. She combed his hair up in a sweep and painted in dark, arching eyebrows. She was masterful. Don went from a harmless-looking, nice guy to the most sinister-looking individual I'd ever seen up close.

That evening changed Don's life in Coburg. He was the hit of the Fasching party, much to the sorrow of his date and creator, who was also an attractive woman, but not the *most* attractive woman. The most attractive woman made such a heavy move on Don that he was somewhat embarrassed, but not so embarrassed that he didn't make a date to see her the next night. That was the beginning of a very hot and heavy romance that lasted all of a couple of weeks, and was soon followed by more of the same. Don had found his groove and was on a roll.

Don studied Russian at the Army Language School and picked up his own brand of German while he was in Coburg. He wasn't a very good Russian linguist, which surprised me, because he was working as a transcriber, and he was an even worse German linguist. His German was sincere, and for the most part, understandable, but only if you also knew at least some English. I don't know if there's such a thing as pidgin German, but if there was, that's what

Don spoke. The women who met Don were willing to overlook that obstacle, because they found him so fascinating.

I was truly interested in the transformation that Don went through after that first party. I wondered why women suddenly found him so compelling. I think it was my introduction to what I now know is the "bad boy" syndrome. There are women who are attracted to bad boys because they believe that these guys, although capable of being mean and nasty, won't be mean to *them* because of their love for them. These same women seem to feel that if a man is kind and nice to them, that means he's probably weak. My theory certainly doesn't apply to *all* women, but there does seem to be this type. The women I dated in Germany usually preferred nice guys, which aligned with my own reputation.

Many of the soldiers in our group played poker. There was a big poker table in the dayroom that would seat about ten guys. Each player ordered $15 or $20 worth of chips. One of the guys had a notebook, and he wrote down the number of chips that each player bought. At the end of the game, or whenever a person dropped out, they would cash in the chips they had, and that would be recorded. At the end of the month, which was payday, the men who were ahead for the month would stand next to the paymaster and collect from the guy with the notebook. Don was always one of the winners.

We were paid in cash, and each of us made about $140 to $175 a month. The first person after the paymaster was the guy with the notebook. Those who were losers for the previous month would pay him first. Then the winners came up and received their winnings.

In most Army units, there was usually a third guy who was the loan shark, but we didn't have one of those in Coburg while I was there.

I set aside the money I needed for basic expenses, which included laundry, cigarettes, and gasoline coupons. I counted out what I thought I'd need for my living expenses for the next four weeks. What I had left, which was usually about $75, I used to play poker. If I won, that meant I could take an extended three-day vacation to Munich or Vienna or somewhere else. If I lost, I would be more or less confined to Coburg for the next four weeks, which was also a pleasant experience. I was a young American in Germany, making good money for the first time in my life.

Don and I became good friends, although he was better educated and more worldly than I was. He also had some quirky traits that set him apart. He liked to take an hour nap after his day shift was over, which many of us did. We'd lie down on our cots, fully clothed, and nap for ten to twenty minutes. Don would change into silk pajamas, close the heavy drapes he'd installed in his room, and sleep for an hour.

When Don was excited, he'd clap the bottom of his hands together like a performing seal. Don and I were in the Pit one evening when a very large German woman entered the bar and approached Don. Apparently, he'd been with this woman one evening and had told some friends about it. Word got back to her, probably with embellishments, and she was angry. She owned a bar herself, which had a German name that the Germans probably used, but to the GIs, it was called Big Mamoo's, which they affectionately called her. She was about six feet tall and had a Rubenesque body with a seductive smile. The story was that her German husband was an SS man who'd fled Germany after the war, and she hadn't wanted to go with him.

She was one of those larger-than-life individuals, which referred to more than just her size. She was generous, spoke passable English, and appeared to genuinely like Americans. She loved life out loud. She wasn't a classically attractive woman, but she had a certain way about her that some of the guys found sexy, especially after a few drinks.

When she saw Don across the dance floor, she headed toward him yelling what she was going to do to him when she got ahold of him. She was about the same height as Don, but she outweighed him by about forty pounds. He knew that the things she was threatening to do to him, she was capable of carrying out, but he figured he was faster than she was, so he danced around the floor and maneuvered toward the door. The whole time he was figuring his escape route, he frantically slapped the bottom of his hands together while rapidly spitting out his pidgin German.

Not only did those of us who watched this theater laugh hysterically, but eventually, so did Big Mamoo. Whatever anger she had, dissipated at the sight of this American soldier performing like a frightened, trained seal. Don quit heading toward the door and said that he'd buy her a drink or two if she promised not to kill him. She agreed, and all was well between them.

Don was Jewish, but most people, especially the Germans, didn't know that. His last name didn't sound Jewish, nor did he make a point of announcing what his background was. This wasn't to say that he was in any way trying to hide the fact, but he was a secular Jew, proud of his heritage, and comfortable with a diverse group of friends. He did have a great interest in the new state of Israel, though. We all read and discussed the book *Exodus* by Leon Uris, which had just been published. We discussed this heroic story over many drinks.

When Don and I double dated, we frequently ended up at a restaurant called Die Oasis. Our favorite food was oxtail soup, which in German is *ochsen schwantze zuppe*. One night, he and I were in the Oasis with two women we'd just met, and he wanted to impress them by ordering in German. The problem was, he left out the word *ochsen*. What he ordered instead was *schwantz* zuppe. *Schwantz* means "tail" in German, and it's also a slang word for *penis*. What Don ordered could have been translated as penis soup.

The waiter looked at him and asked politely, "Whose?"

The two women and I found the entire exchange quite funny, as did the waiter. Don was initially perplexed, until he thought about what the waiter had asked. It then became one of Don's favorite stories.

The girl who was Don's date was named Karen. It turned out that her family was German aristocracy. Her father, who'd been killed in the war, was a baron. Don dated Karen for almost two months, which was longer than most of his romances.

One evening when a group of us were drinking in a bar, someone asked Don if Karen knew he was Jewish. He thought about it for a moment and said, "No, I don't think so." That prompted a long discussion among us as to whether or not Don should tell her before Karen got in any deeper.

Don said, "On the one hand, why should I have to tell the women I date that I'm Jewish? On the other hand, if we fall in love, it will become an issue. If not for us, it will undoubtedly be an issue for my parents and probably for hers, especially since her father was killed in the war."

It was a standing joke among us that if we met a German whose father was killed in the war, he must have been killed by the Americans.

If the father were alive, he fought against the Russians. We concluded that the Americans were much better shots than the Russians.

Van Stry said to Don, "You have to tell her, because if you marry Karen, you'll be a baron, but if she marries you, she'll be a Jew."

I think Don could have been offended by that comment, except that it came from Van Stry, who was one of his very good friends. Van Stry was always joking or teasing. We sometimes called him Bubbles because of his effervescent personality. He was from New York and wanted to be in theater, and his goal in life was to appear in *Pal Joey* on Broadway. If we'd known what the phrase meant at the time, we would have described him as being hyperkinetic.

There was one incident in which Van Stry was driving his car back from a bar to the Kaserne. He was from New York and didn't learn how to drive until he got into the Army. Better said, he didn't start driving until he was in the Army. Many of us felt that he never really learned how to drive, and being with him in a car was always an adventure. That rainy night as we approached the turnoff from the main road to the Kaserne, he took the turn too sharply. The car tipped over on its side and slid for about thirty yards before it stopped in front of the gate. None of us were seriously hurt and only sustained a couple of bruises. We got help from the soldiers inside the Kaserne, who turned the car upright so we could drive in. I believe I drove. The guard at the gate reported us, and we all received Article 15's, which restricted us to the barracks for a week, when we weren't working.

Van Stry took advantage of this opportunity. He told us we'd all perform the musical *Pal Joey*. He brought in some Canadian Club and Chivas Regal with ice cubes, and we rehearsed in the hallway outside our rooms. It was surprising how good our make-shift cast became. Some of the guys could sing, and a couple of them could dance. Of course, Van Stry was the star, and the memory of him singing the hit tunes from *Pal Joey* has stuck with me. None of us actually looked upon that week as punishment, but rather a rehearsal for future stardom for at least one of us.

While Don was in Coburg, he received a very tragic letter from his mother, telling him that his older brother, who was in the Air Force, had died in a plane crash. Don worshiped his older brother, as did everyone who knew him. He was the star in the family, which took the pressure off of Don. Don didn't have to get all As in school. He could get by with Bs, and even flirt with being a rebel. He didn't dress like a hippie, but his favorite author was Jack Kerouac, and his favorite book was *On the Road*, which he read twice while at the Language School. He also carried a copy of Kant's *Critique of Pure Reason*; he confided to me that he never read it, but periodically moved the bookmark farther along.

Soon after his brother's tragic death, he received a letter from his mother, telling him that it was time for him to become "a nice Jewish boy." I was told, when he got that letter, that he immediately sat down and wrote a letter to his mother. He wrote ten times in big block letters:

"I am not a nice Jewish boy."

He told me that he didn't want to hurt his parents, nor was he in any way ashamed of being Jewish. He just didn't want to be put in a role that was not of his choosing.

He wasn't religious, nor were his parents, but they did live in a Jewish community, and they, along with their friends, had high expectations for their children. First of all, he knew that his parents would put pressure on him to marry a Jewish girl, and Don didn't want to limit his options. Second, he was expected to go into a profession that would allow him to support his family in a manner that was consistent with the way he'd been raised.

Don grew up in an upper middle class, predominantly Jewish suburb outside of Philadelphia, which is one of the things that he rebelled against. After the Army, he intended to live in Greenwich Village in New York City, or maybe in Paris. He wanted to write, if not the Great American novel, at least one as good as Norman Mailer's. I watched Don anguish over his dilemma, but I ultimately felt that he was going to follow his mother's wishes. He was too nice of a guy not to.

One of the many things Don tried to teach me was how to dine. He noticed that my palate was relatively limited. Although it wasn't required in the mess hall, my dining habits weren't up to his standards. Prior to the Army, I hadn't eaten in good restaurants more than three or four times in my life.

The best restaurant in Coburg was near the train station. Don said he wanted me to go with him to dinner at this establishment. He'd won quite a bit at poker that month, so he said that the meal would be on him. He told me that I had to wear a sport coat and a tie, and we were going to dine at 8:00 p.m. that Friday evening.

When we both showed up, we were seated by a waiter in a tuxedo. Don said that he'd do all the ordering for both of us, which I felt was going to be a challenge. I reminded him that a peanut butter and banana sandwich was my idea of exotic food, and although the variation of foods that I'd tried was 100 times more diverse since I'd joined the Army, there were still some I wouldn't try.

He asked, "Like what?"

"Cottage cheese," I said.

He asked, "You don't like the taste of cottage cheese?"

I said, "I don't know. I've never tasted cottage cheese." Then I clarified: "My problem is, I don't like the *looks* of cottage cheese."

When I was about nine years old, my brother and I sat down to dinner, and my mother tried to give us some cottage cheese. I looked at it and asked my mom, "Am I supposed to eat this, or have I already?"

That was probably the only time my brother felt kindly toward me. After that remark, he got up and said, "I'm sorry, but I'm no longer hungry."

Don said, "After that story, you can be sure that I will not order cottage cheese. In fact, I'll check with you on what I'm going to order, but I hope you'll be open to trying other things, especially those that are more pleasant to the eye."

The first thing he ordered was a very nice wine. It was a German Mosel that was light and fruity. He then ordered an appetizer plate of sausages and cheeses. I loved the sausages, and even ate some of the cheeses, because none of it was runny. For a main dish, he ordered steak with pommes frites, with a small Caesar salad. He ordered the steaks rare, with a red wine to be served with them. I devoured my steak and more than my fair share of pommes frites. I was going to ask for ketchup, but the waiter intimidated me. I also ate most of the salad and felt quite proud of myself.

We then had a glorious dessert that was some type of German pie made of fruits and pastry, topped with Italian ice cream. We finished the meal with a small snifter of cognac. I was completely satisfied, and proud of the fact that I'd used the right utensils for each course. I was helped by the waiter and his three sons, all of whom were dressed in tuxedos, including the youngest one, who couldn't have been older than ten. His sole job was to light our cigarettes.

When we were through, the headwaiter asked Don if there would be anything else. Don paused for about thirty seconds, looked at me and smiled, and said, "Yes, we'd like the entire meal once again."

The waiter didn't hesitate. He produced the Mosel wine that we started with and placed the order for the rest of the meal. I believe we didn't leave the restaurant until 11:30 p.m. I knew that I'd never enjoy any meal as much as I enjoyed that one, and I was sure I'd never have a meal like that again.

I don't know how much the dinner cost, because Don wouldn't tell me. However, he seemed very pleased with both the meal and himself. I was grateful and stuffed. When I look back on that night, I have to smile, because it's a perfect example of why Americans tend to be more overweight than Germans. When a German is asked if he'd like more food, his answer is, "No, I'm satisfied," but the American says, "No, I'm full. I was satisfied after the first meal, but I ate until I was full."

Vienna, Austria

In June of 1959, Don and three others were transferred to a post outside of Passau, Germany, which is on the Danube River, east of Munich. They joined a group of other ASA soldiers who were living in an old farmhouse. This was called "living on the economy," because they had to pay rent and buy their own food. Consequently, the Army paid them extra money that always amounted to more than their actual expenses. It turned out to be a very good deal, which helped them get over leaving Coburg and their friends.

Don and I continued our friendship, even though it was about 220 miles from Coburg to Passau. He came up to Coburg a couple of times, and I went to Passau a few times, but our most memorable meeting was in Vienna.

I had an extended three-day pass and met Don at the train station in Vienna on a Friday afternoon. He had two attractive American girls with him. They were both students at the American University in Vienna, and Don had met them through Bob. Bob had received a letter from a mutual friend back home, who'd told him that one of our classmates from Royal Oak High School was studying in Vienna. Her name was Claudia, and Bob arranged to meet her on a trip to Vienna with Don. Claudia brought along a friend named Donna, who quickly fell in love with Don. Claudia and Bob were just friends, so Don didn't feel like he was betraying anything when he brought her along to be my date. Although we'd both attended Royal Oak, I'd never met Claudia for a number of reasons, one of which was that I'd been known as a hoodlum. Claudia was a good girl. She didn't know my name; otherwise, she might not have come along.

After the introduction at the train station, Don suggested that we have lunch, which normally wouldn't be something I'd remember. But this turned out to be a special lunch for two reasons. The first was that Don ordered creamed spinach for everyone. I knew that he was still trying to make me worldlier, but I figured I'd draw the line at creamed spinach. I didn't eat creamed *anything*, even corn, and I loved corn. I didn't imagine there'd be any way I could ever stomach creamed spinach when I detested spinach, period.

Don, in his charming fashion, convinced all of us that this was the best creamed spinach in the world, and one of the top three dishes he'd ever tasted. The two girls weren't that enthusiastic about spinach either, but Don was a hard person to deny or defy. We each timidly took a forkful of creamed spinach and cautiously ate it. We looked at one another with unexpected joy. It was delicious. In fact, I've never forgotten how good it was. This, paradoxically, worked against Don's goal of making me appreciate the finer things, because since then, I've never found creamed spinach that even came close to being as delicious as that first serving.

After an exceptionally fine lunch, Don told me what we were going to do on my three-day pass. After checking me in to the hotel where we were all staying, we were going to walk around downtown Vienna and eventually have dinner at a restaurant near the opera house. The reason why we were going to dine there was that it was world famous for its pastries. Then we were going to the opera.

I asked if I could see Don privately for a moment. He smiled, looked at me, and asked, "What's the matter?"

I told him, "You just introduced me to a very attractive girl, and *you* are with a very attractive girl, so why are we going to the opera? Shouldn't we go to a nightclub where they serve drinks, and we can laugh and have fun together?"

He said, "You may do as you wish and we will meet you afterward, but the three of us are going to the opera to see *La Bohème*."

I knew when I was beaten, so I said okay, but I wasn't happy.

After another great meal and an even greater dessert called a Sacher-Torte, we crossed the street and entered the Vienna State Opera House. Don said that this was the second-best opera house in the world next to La Scala in Milan. I thought, *At least this misadventure will have some story value.*

Don bought the best tickets in the house, which were in a

private loge that had two sofas. We were on the second-floor balcony, which extended out over the first floor so that when we looked down, we were about the eighth-row center, or so it seemed. We could see the entire stage, and being in the center, I assumed the acoustics would be fabulous.

From the beginning of the opera, I was spellbound. The sights, the voices, and the music were overwhelming. Don had told me over dinner that the opera had been written by Puccini. He was aware that I knew nothing about opera and even less about Puccini. He explained to me that Puccini had written this when he was a relatively young man, and he'd written the story, the dialogue, and the music for each voice and each instrument.

My mother made me take piano lessons for two years when I was about nine years old. I hated to practice, and my teacher hated trying to teach me. During those two years, I learned how to read music, and I learned how to play three songs from memory. Much to the delight of my teacher and me, my mother let me quit after two years.

My taste in music was more eclectic. For some reason, I memorized most of the songs I heard on the hit parade during the '40s. During the '50s, my friends and I listened to a station out of Nashville that we could only get on our car radios in a place we called Beer Hill. They played two types of music: rhythm and blues, which we called R&B and was sung by African Americans; and country and western, which some called hillbilly music and was sung by Caucasian singers.

My favorite album at that time, which is still one of my top ten today, was *Ray Charles Sings Country and Western*. The album has lyrics that I love, which are sad and sentimental, and is in the style that is uniquely Ray Charles.

Don was thrilled that I was enjoying the opera. During the two intermissions, I gushed over it, and I think the girls enjoyed it, too. It was fun for him to introduce all of us to an art form that he loved and see that we were appreciating it as well.

After the opera, we went to a nightclub. Don started to tell us what we were going to do the next night, and I looked at him and said, "Don, you just gave me one of the best experiences of my life. I noticed on the way out of the opera house that they have an opera tomorrow night call *Don Giovanni*, by Mozart. Whatever you have planned couldn't possibly be as exciting for me as seeing *Don Giovanni*."

Don laughed and said, "I don't like being overruled, and I like it even less when my plans are thwarted, but this time, I'll let you win."

That trip to Vienna introduced me to two of the best operas ever created, performed in the second-best opera house in the world. I've since tried to pass on that experience to others, and to duplicate it as often as I can. I've come close, but those two evenings will remain special to me for as long as I'm here.

CHAPTER 6

Coburg Once Again

When I went back to Coburg, I looked up Dave Smith, who was a friend of Don's. Dave was three years older than I was and a hundred times better educated. I assumed that he knew something about opera, so I told him about my experience. He was surprised to hear that Don had insisted we go to the opera, because Dave had gone to the opera in Coburg a couple of times, and Don never wanted to join him.

As it turns out, Dave was a real opera lover and taught me how to truly enjoy it. He had recordings of *La Bohème* and *Don Giovanni*, and they both came with printed versions of the libretto, which is the written dialogue. Dick and I shared our apartment with two other friends, and one had a very good Gründig record player. David and I sat for long periods of time, listening to the recordings of those two operas, and following along with the librettos.

I was a little disappointed as I read the translations of some of the songs. I was and still am especially taken by the aria "Mi Chiamo Mimi" in *La Bohème*, but when it was translated into English, it lost some of its beauty. Watching it and listening to it in Italian was more romantic than words, such as, "They call me Mimi. I don't know why. I make lunch."

Dave and I went to the opera a couple of times in Coburg. It wasn't the second-best opera house in the world, but it did present me with the opportunity to hear a number of operas, the most memorable being *Fidelio*, by Beethoven. That was the only opera he wrote. I liked it even more after Dave and I went over the libretto and listened to a recording, but it didn't stir me in the same way that Puccini, Verdi, or Mozart did.

☆ ☆ ☆

The last girl Don dated in Coburg before his transfer to Passau was an attractive and very charming woman named Rosi. Dave occasionally joined the two of them when they went to dinner. Don's interest in Rosi never reached a fever level, so when he was transferred to Passau, he wasn't heartbroken. Dave, being a kind and thoughtful friend, still felt it necessary to ask Don if he minded if he took out Rosi. Apparently, on those occasions when the three of them were together, Dave had fallen madly in love with her.

Dave did not express that love immediately, but he did have lunch and coffee dates with Rosi in an attempt to explain to her that she didn't cause the end of the relationship with Don. Without betraying his friend, Dave explained to Rosi that Don was not at the point in his life where he was willing or able to fall in love for keeps. Once Dave felt that Rosi understood and accepted what happened, he explained to her that everything he'd said about Don was absolutely true. On the other hand, he was two years older than Don, had finished college, and was ready and able to fall in love. In fact, he *had* fallen in love with her.

I think it took Rosi a while to realize what a fortunate person she was, and what an outstanding individual Dave was, but eventually she did. They arranged to get married in Coburg. Luckily, Dave had enough time left to file all the necessary papers and get them back before he had to rotate back to the United States.

I believe that Rosi was the only girl Dave dated in Germany. He was different from Don and me—he was shy and serious, although he had a sharp and sardonic sense of humor. He seemed to be somewhat uncomfortable in his own body. He had the same awkward look that a very tall person or a large puppy might have. He had dark, wavy hair and eyes that were extremely kind and trusting. He seemed to have no desire to be a ladies' man. He met Rosi through Don and fell in love, which turned out extremely well for both of them.

The Germans require people to have a civil ceremony in order to be legally married. Most people also have a church ceremony. David asked me to be his best man, and I felt quite honored. The civil ceremony took place at the City Hall in what would be the equivalent of a magistrate's office. Dave, Rosi, her bridesmaid, and I sat on four chairs in front of the magistrate's desk. He asked David and Rosi a series of questions, and then gave them some advice, which I've never forgotten. At the time, I thought it was a little too Germanic, but over the years, I've learned to appreciate the wisdom of his message.

The magistrate looked at Dave and said, "If Rosi isn't the first person you go to when you experience something wonderful, or isn't the first person you go to when you're hurt or in need, then perhaps you should think this over."

He then looked at Rosi and said the same thing. He added, "There are many reasons why two people may be attracted to one another, but if a marriage is going to last, the two people must become best friends. When two people are going to live together and raise a family together, that means they not only have to love one another, but they also have to know, trust, and respect one another. They have to want to spend most of their time together, and they must learn to cherish their relationship most of all."

When I walked out of there, I mentioned that I'd found his advice to be a little too practical. Rosi and her bridesmaid were familiar with the ceremony and knew what they were going to hear. Dave understood what the man was saying better than I did, but then again, as he so often reminded me, I was just a kid.

The church service was primarily for the benefit of Rosi's parents. None of the other participants were that excited about it. Fortunately, it was relatively short and ended up being somewhat amusing. David asked a number of us to attend, including Don and Van Stry, who were both in Passau. Dave didn't think they'd come, but he felt that it would be the right thing to do to invite them. The invitation gave them a chance to send a card and/or a present. To our surprise, Don and Van Stry both showed up.

The only other people in the church were Rosi's family and some of her friends. When the priest addressed Dave and Rosi and offered his advice about their relationship to God and the Church, he looked in vain for their eyes, all four of which were cast downward. Dave and Rosi weren't religious. Van Stry was a fallen-away Catholic, and Don was a nonpracticing Jew. And according to my former Baptist brethren, I was an infidel. After searching in vain for some contact with any one of us, the minister gave up. He eventually raised his arms and eyes upward, and offered his blessings to the ceiling.

Rosi's family had a wonderful reception, with good food and wine, and a legitimate sense of happiness for their daughter. The evening was going along very well when, at one point, Don, having consumed enough liquid courage, decided that he'd give a speech. Most of the people at the reception, including Rosi's parents, knew that Don and Rosi had gone out together. I wondered how Don, with his limited German, was going to navigate this rather delicate terrain.

We all agreed that he ended up doing quite well. There was one sentence in which he mentioned how well he knew Rosi. He referenced what a fine person she was. The literal translation was, "Believe me, Rosie is good, really good, and I know Rosi really, really well." That could've been misunderstood, but I believe the majority of the guests chose the more benign interpretation.

The manner in which Rosi's parents handled her relationship with Dave and their ultimate marriage was the exception and not the rule. There was a stigma attached to dating American soldiers. German men of marrying age frequently referred to any German woman who dated a GI as an Ami Mädchen. *Ami* was short for "American," and *Mädchen* was the German word for "girl."

The label didn't have a good connotation among Germans, and I don't think this bias was misplaced. American soldiers overseas weren't always our best ambassadors. Most of them didn't speak any German or try to learn the language. Most of them were young and away from home for the first time, and some thought they'd personally won the war. The ASA in Coburg was different. I was among the youngest and least educated. We all spoke either German or Russian, and many of us spoke other languages as well.

I walked into the latrine one day while four guys were cleaning the toilets in preparation for one of our infrequent inspections. They were all laughing, which wasn't a normal accompaniment to cleaning toilets. I asked what was so funny.

One of them said, "We just realized that among the four of us, we have over twenty-five years of college education and six degrees."

Dave was one of those four guys.

Paris, France

I took my first leave in Europe shortly after I returned to Coburg. One of the guys on my trick and I decided to drive to Paris and spend ten days there. His name was Kerry Belcher, and he was from California. Kerry was about 6'2" tall, blonde, and blue-eyed. He didn't speak any German and was somewhat shy and soft-spoken, but he was a good guy and interesting, once you got him into a conversation.

We took a train to Coburg, picked up his car, and made our way toward Paris. Kerry made it very clear that he was going to do all the driving, and that was all right with me. The weather was cool, but we still had the convertible top down. I felt like I was off on a new and special adventure. As it turned out, I was right.

We arrived in Paris in the late afternoon. We'd reserved a room in a small hotel that we had trouble finding. Kerry didn't speak French, and neither did I. Asking French people for help in English was getting us nothing but shrugs, so I tried asking for the hotel address in my version of French. People understood my question, but I couldn't understand their responses, since they were in French. While responding, they also pointed in a certain direction, and we drove that way for a distance, then stopped and asked someone else.

We drove around for about forty-five minutes before we found our hotel. I'm from Detroit, and I'm a very good driver. Kerry was from Los Angeles, and he was also a good driver, but more fearless than me. Neither of us could quite decipher the French rules for driving in

Paris, except that they included frequent use of the horn. Kerry managed to remain completely calm throughout the entire ordeal. I concluded that he either had nerves of steel or no nerves at all.

After we found the hotel and checked in to our room, we walked over to a restaurant. I was extremely excited to be in Paris. I'd read some books on existentialism and was completely enamored with Jean-Paul Sartre and Albert Camus. I'd read somewhere that both men had spent quite a bit of their time in the café Les Deux Magots, and I was eager to go there.

I explained all of this to Kerry, but noticed he wasn't responding. I looked into his eyes and realized that none of this was of any interest to him. I stopped in midsentence and asked if he wanted to go back to the hotel.

He smiled and said, "Sure."

I thought, *This isn't going to work.* I needed to either find someone who shared my interests or be alone. My dilemma was, I was there with Kerry, and I wanted him to also enjoy his time in Paris.

The next day, we went to the Louvre Museum. I was sure Kerry wanted to see one of the greatest collections of masterpieces in the world, as did I, but I also had an ulterior motive. The Louvre was full of good-looking women, most of whom were tourists, and some of whom, I hoped, spoke English. After about twenty minutes, I saw a very attractive young woman. I heard her speaking Austrian German and realized that might be even better. I approached her, and we struck up a conversation. I introduced her to Kerry and saw that she was instantly attracted to him. That was a good start.

After touring the museum, I suggested that we go to the Eiffel Tower and drive in Kerry's car. Once she saw his Austin Healey, I knew I was almost home. While walking around the Eiffel Tower,

I'd mentioned to her that the reason Kerry hadn't said much was that he didn't speak German. I also told her he was very interested in her.

She said, "I like him, too. I can understand a little English, so we should have no problem."

The three of us had dinner that night in an Italian restaurant and made arrangements to go our separate ways the next day. Then she said something to me that I'd never heard before. She told me that I spoke very good German, but unfortunately, my accent reflected my personality. I asked what that meant.

She said, "Your accent is Prussian and arrogant."

Most of the German teachers at the Language School were north Germans, as are Prussians, and many Austrians feel that all Germans are arrogant, but I believe that her comment was really aimed at Americans, even German-speaking Americans. Apparently, she was willing to make an exception if the American was rich.

The next day, I left the hotel before Kerry got up and started searching for Les Deux Magots. I wandered the streets of Paris for most of the day and became somewhat discouraged. I finally found the café in the late afternoon. I wondered if being alone in Paris was better than being with Kerry.

I walked into the café and sat at a table by myself. I ordered a coffee and took out my pack of American cigarettes. I was feeling a little sorry for myself, and not a bit existential, when a gentleman approached my table and, in accented English, asked me if I knew where the American Express office was. As it happened, I'd been there earlier to see if I had any mail. I'd told my mother that I was going to Paris, and that if she wanted to contact me, she should send a letter or telegram to the American Express office.

After I told the gentleman where the American Express office was, he asked me if I wanted to join him and his friend for a drink.

I said, "Yes, thank you. I never knew a person could feel so lonely in Paris."

He was French, and his friend was a Canadian, so the language we used among the three of us was English. The Canadian worked for the BBC, and he wanted to know my impressions of France, particularly Paris. He had a portable tape recorder and was recording our conversation.

This was the era when Americans' image in Europe was at a low point. The book *The Ugly American* expressed all the common complaints heard about American tourists. The French had a reputation, especially the Parisians, of being the least accommodating Europeans.

As we talked, I noticed that two women sitting at the table next to us were laughing each time we said something funny. I leaned over at one point and said, "You obviously speak English," and asked them to join us, which they did. I couldn't tell from their accents what their nationalities were, so I asked. They were both from Israel, and were native-born Israelis. A little later in our conversation, which was quite interesting, one of the ladies leaned over and said something to her friend in Hebrew. They both smiled. I asked them what they were smiling about.

One of them said, "You wouldn't believe me if I told you."

I said, "Try me."

She said, "When you walked in, my friend said to me, he is an American, a corporal in the Army, and he and I are going to spend the next week together."

The three of us were all taken aback by that comment. We

argued that I looked more Scandinavian than American. I was wearing clothes that I'd bought in Europe. The Frenchman said he'd addressed me in English when he first approached my table because he knew all Scandinavians spoke English. He was surprised when he heard my American accent. All three of us agreed that we had no idea what a corporal looked like. And we all felt that spending a week with this charming lady would probably do wonders for my loneliness.

I did spend the next week with the woman. Her name was Shula Schön, and she was born in Tel Aviv. She was about six years older than me, and was one of the most fascinating people I've ever met. She spoke five languages. I can't comment on how proficient she was at the other three, but her English and German were delightful and charming. She wasn't classically beautiful, but she had such a pleasant smile and infectious laugh, that I found her very attractive. Her figure would meet the definition of *zaftig* perfectly, which seemed appropriate. We arranged to meet the next day at the Louvre.

Shula led me to all of her favorite pieces of art in the museum. Along the way, I found out that she was engaged to a man who was about ten years older than she was. I also discovered that she had a very impish sense of humor.

When we looked at a particular painting, and if there were other people around, she would listen to their language. If it were one that she also spoke, she'd say something to me like, "Let's go back to the hotel after this painting and make wild gypsy love."

I didn't know what she was saying, but the people around me did. They'd look at me with either shock or envy, and I'd have to ask her what she'd said. After her translation, I asked, "Is that a real suggestion on your part, or is this for fun?"

She smiled and said, "You'll find out."

After the Louvre, we had lunch in a little café nearby. She started what turned out to be the most mystifying conversation I'd ever had. She said, "You just finished reading *The Fountainhead* by Ayn Rand, right?"

I looked at her and asked, "How could you possibly know that?"

She said, "I know a lot about you."

She then told me about my ambitions, my fears, and my insecurities. I didn't know how to respond. I'm a candid and open individual, but there are certain things I keep to myself, especially things that have to do with my fears and insecurities. I was completely shocked that this Israeli woman, whom I'd just met, had such insights into my secret thoughts.

We spent the afternoon at Versailles, at her insistence, which was awe-inspiring. But it was difficult for me to concentrate completely on what I was seeing, because I was still spooked by what she'd told me. She'd offer an opinion about something we saw, and then say, "But you agree with that," or "You don't agree with that," and she was always right.

On the way back from Versailles, she started telling me about herself. She'd been a fifteen-year-old girl when Israel was declared an independent country. Three years later, she was in the military and experienced the Second Arab War. She had strong opinions about Israel, Jews, and the Middle East.

I was raised a few blocks away from a predominantly Jewish neighborhood that was wealthier than mine, but we all went to the same school. I knew and made friends with a number of Jewish kids. I even took Jewish holidays off from school, and with my last name being Teachman, I felt I could get away with it. I did succeed my first year, but midway into the second year, the woodshop teacher became suspicious.

He asked, "Teachman, why were you absent yesterday?"

I said, "It was a holiday."

He said, "Only if you're Jewish. Are you Jewish?"

"No, sir," I confessed, "but I'm very tolerant." That ended my extra days off.

I heard anti-Semitic comments from many people around me, including some of my friends and family. But my father always expressed great admiration for his Jewish friends, and my mother loved everybody except bigots.

When I turned thirteen, my father said to me, "In the Jewish tradition, a boy becomes a man at thirteen." Then he said, "Although we're not Jewish, today you are a man."

I asked him, "What does that mean?"

I was entering my hoodlum-wannabe stage, and I stayed out later than I was supposed to a few times. My mother would chastise me when I came home.

My father said to me, "Part of being a man is that you no longer have to report to us where you're going, what you're doing, or when you're coming home."

I smiled. "Okay, what's the downside?"

He said, "We will pay your room and board for as long as you're in school."

I said, "You already do that. Does this new freedom include buying my clothes and stuff?"

He smiled and said, "No, just your room and board."

I asked, "How do I buy my clothes and things like that?"

He answered, "You're going to have to get a job."

I looked at my father and said, "I have a lot of Jewish friends who just turned thirteen. That's not what they got for their thirteenth birthday. They got blue sapphire rings, bonds, and savings accounts from their relatives for their college education. And none of them had to get a job."

My father looked at me and smiled again. "I told you, we're not Jewish."

Shula asked me if I knew where we could get a hamburger. I asked why she wanted one. She said she'd always heard about Americans and their hamburgers, and she just wanted to experience one.

I took her to a restaurant that served hamburgers, and we each ordered one. It arrived open-faced. On one side of the bun was lettuce and a slice of tomato. On the other side of the bun was a medium-rare hamburger. I asked if they had ketchup, and they did. I put some on my hamburger and started to put the one bun on top of the other when Shula asked, "What are you doing?"

I said, "I'm going to eat my hamburger."

"You don't eat food with your hands," she said.

Then I said, "No one eats a hamburger with a knife and fork."

She smiled, "In front of me they do."

I ate my hamburger with a knife and fork for the first and only time in my life, as did she.

After a couple of bites, I asked if she liked it. She shrugged. "I don't know what all the fuss is about. Besides, it's difficult to eat."

I said, "Not if you pick it up and eat it like you're supposed to."

She glared at me. "I'll have to take your word for that, because I will never try to eat something that big with my hands."

I walked her back to her hotel after dinner, and she continued to tell me things about myself, things I'd never told anybody. We shook hands and I said goodbye. On the way back to my hotel, I wondered if I was supposed to try to kiss her. It hadn't crossed my mind, but I thought, *She's an attractive woman, and I think she likes me.* Maybe she thought I'm not attracted to her. On the other hand, she was engaged, and if I tried to kiss her, she might have found that offensive.

The next morning, we were going to meet for breakfast. I got to the hotel, and the concierge handed me a note that said, "Please come up to the room."

I got to Shula's room and knocked on the door. She asked who it was, and I told her. She said, "Come on in, the door's open."

I walked into the room, and she was in bed. She smiled and said, "Please join me."

I went to get on the bed, and she said, "No, get undressed."

Getting undressed in front of a woman in a fully lighted room wasn't a common experience for me. I wasn't sure how I was going to react. I thought if I got excited, she might be upset, or worse yet, disappointed. If I *didn't* get excited, I would be embarrassed, and she might be offended. I figured this was a no-win situation for me, but I had no choice. I got undressed as quickly as I could and crawled into bed. She was also nude. She put her arms around me and kissed me. After a few more kisses, she pulled away from me, smiled, and said, "You're uncomfortable, aren't you?"

I said, "Yes, I am, and I don't know why."

She said, "Don't be. Nothing sexual is going to happen, because it's not supposed to happen. Let's get dressed."

We both got dressed with our backs to one another. As we walked to the restaurant, I said, "I don't know what's going on. Did I do something wrong?"

"No, not at all," she said. "I wanted to prove to you that this isn't that kind of a relationship. We were meant to meet, because I have something to give you that you need. This will happen again with other people, but it will never be sexual. It is spiritual, but not in the religious sense. There are people you will meet whom you are supposed to meet. They will know you, and they will reaffirm who you are and what you're doing. They can be men or women, but they will always be older than you. Consider them your guides who are giving you strength and direction."

I didn't know what to say. We reached the restaurant and ordered something to eat. I kept staring at her.

She said, "Now that that's out of the way, let's really enjoy the next six days," which we did.

During those days, Shula filled me with stories about Israel and her life. We explored and experienced Paris together. We hugged and kissed a few times, but nothing more than that. She teased me quite a bit about my innocence and inexperience. I laughed, learned, and loved every minute of it.

On our last day, she gave me her brother's address, which was a kibbutz (a farm in Israel) near Jerusalem. She said that I'd like her brother, who was just a year older than me, and that I'd love spending time on a kibbutz. We kissed and said goodbye.

I asked, "What about your address? Can I visit you, too?"

"Of, course," she said, "but you know that's probably not going to happen." I nodded and walked back toward my hotel. I had tears in my eyes, but I was smiling. I knew that I'd just had a life-changing experience, but I wasn't sure why. I found myself singing a refrain from a song she'd sung to me in German the day before; the song—whose author I can't recall—reflected on a simple flirtation that feels like love but is an illusion that is quickly over, but, in time, becomes a beautiful memory.

A Return to Coburg

I was in the latrine getting ready to go on my day shift when a new guy walked in. We were expecting a new staff sergeant, but one glance told me this wasn't him. He was about 5'6" tall and a little chubby, with blonde hair that was longer than regulations allowed. He had on GI boxer underwear and a pair of suede Wellington boots. He had a mezuzah on a chain around his neck, and a tattoo of a panther that covered most of his right shoulder. He wore brown horn-rimmed glasses that accentuated his rather large nose.

I thought, *I know I'm going to like this guy. I hope they assign him to our trick*, and they did.

His name was Michael Holquist, and he was from Rockford, Illinois. When Mike arrived, I had just about a year to go in my enlistment. We became good friends and stayed pals until he passed away at the age of 80. He was three years older than me, and prior to the Army, he'd attended the University of Illinois for a period of time—but I was never clear about how long.

There was a lot about Mike's life that wasn't clear. He talked about having some psychological problems when he was young, though he never exactly said so. It appeared that the root of his problems was his genius IQ. When Mike was fifteen, one enlightened psychiatrist concluded that he was bored being in the ninth grade. He recommended that instead of being sent to an institution because of his problems adjusting, Mike should attend college classes. His parents enrolled him in the University of Illinois.

Michael told me that at the university he had a group of friends who all wore black berets, except Michael, who wore a white beret. They would all enroll in the same classes, primarily literature and political science courses, and Michael would constantly challenge the professors. The good professors were intrigued; the bad ones were incensed.

He was the most knowledgeable individual I'd ever met, which at that time wasn't saying much, but I can still make that comment today. It was soon evident that he was more knowledgeable than any of us in Coburg. We had two PhDs among us: one in science and one in history. Mike could discuss any subject with anybody, and he was very good at it.

I remembered one discussion, specifically, in which he was arguing politics with the PhD in history, a guy named Ron Casagrande, who later went into the State Department as a Foreign Service officer. Ron was also very well spoken. Mike made a contention that Ron disagreed with somewhat caustically. Mike looked at him and said:

"Without stooping to sarcasm, I will respond to your comments," and proceeded to give him a ten-minute speech.

Dick and I were sitting there, and we almost applauded.

I found out in my discussions with Mike that he'd won a prize in poetry at the University of Illinois. I also learned that he was an artist and could draw very well.

Ultimately, I was glad to discover that there were some things that Mike couldn't do. We all played cards—usually Hearts—while working the swing and midnight shifts. Mike was one of the worst card players I'd ever seen and definitely the worst Hearts player. Each time he made a dumb play, he got up and jumped around, all the while berating his stupid mistake. Eventually we all caught on and told him to spare us the dramatics. We knew that these weren't mistakes, because he made them over and over. The truth was, he never concentrated on the game. His mind was always elsewhere.

Mike was engaged to a woman in Chicago, and he sent for her to come to Germany to get married. Her name was Lydia, and it took her about six months to come over. Lydia was also super bright and well educated. She was a little taller than Mike and also wore glasses. I liked her immediately. She had me over for dinner a number of times, which I knew was her idea rather than Mike's. He liked me, but he didn't find me intellectually challenging, and for Mike, this meant that spending time with me was nonproductive.

Mike liked good wine, good food, and good conversation. I knew nothing about wine. I was only beginning to learn a little about good food, and whatever conversations we had consisted of him talking and me listening and learning. I once gave a little-longer-than-normal response to something he said, and he told me:

"Teachman, the only way I'm going to believe that you had one year of college is if you tell me that English is your second language."

Some people would have been hurt by a comment like that, but I grew up being teased by my father, my brother, and many of my friends. I quickly learned to distinguish between good teasing and bad teasing. I still feel that Mike's line was one of the funniest things anybody has ever said about me. I confess to using it myself on other deserving people. I usually attribute it to Mike, but not always.

Mike convinced me that my West Side Detroit dialect was a liability. I'd already realized that my grammar was skewed, but I picked up a larger vocabulary just by hanging around Dick and some of the other guys in my company. However, after Mike's comment, I dedicated myself to improving my language skills. My dedication turned out to be a lifelong pursuit.

Before Lydia arrived, I went to a couple of Fasching parties with Mike. After a couple of drinks, he let loose a bit and became very funny. He even enjoyed being a little silly. The rest of the time, he took life very seriously.

He questioned my lifestyle, saying that I wasted too much time pursuing what he thought were frivolous endeavors. I remember him saying, "You're wasting so much time being friends to some people who are never going to help you achieve what you need to achieve."

I was a little offended by that comment and attempted to defend my lifestyle. I told him that friendship was very important to me, and I thought that it should be important to everybody. Mike agreed, but he said that it was important to choose your friends wisely. I found that to be a little snooty. There was nothing mean about Mike, and everybody liked him. It was just difficult to accept his position that every minute of every day, you had to be getting better educated.

Years later, Mike said that the major difference between us academically was that I gathered knowledge in order to be able to share it and connect with people, which would make me an effective teacher. He, on the other hand, gathered knowledge in order to always be the smartest guy in the room. This qualified him as a scholar, and, he acknowledged, somewhat of a pedant in the classroom.

I later found out that he joined the Army because he was kicked out of college—on what grounds, I'm not sure, but I think it was for political activism. He moved to Chicago and worked at various jobs for two years. He said he had a penchant for taller women, and he went into bars with his friends to pick fights. I asked him how many he won, and he said none, but his friends stopped him from getting killed. And his tall girlfriends would offer him sympathy while nursing him back to health.

While he was at the Army Language School, he found a challenge that changed his life forever. He loved studying languages, especially Russian. He was so proficient at the language, that near the end of his course of study at the Language School, he was asked to translate a number of Russian songs into English. His previous love of literature and poetry helped him to not only present accurate translations, but beautiful ones as well. Russian became Michael's lifelong passion and his profession.

In one of our many conversations in Coburg, Mike gave me a gift that I've attempted to pass on to all of my students. He said that knowledge alone isn't enough. It should lead to wisdom, and the beginning of wisdom is recognizing that we know nothing. The next step is to recognize that we can never know anything for sure. And the hardest part is, in spite of that lack of certainty, to accept the fact that we still have to make decisions.

Michael had already made a few life-or-death decisions, because he was an extremely troubled young man. At that point, I had made none. I found his formula interesting, but not earth-shattering. A few years after I left the Army, when I was married with a son and studying philosophy at the university, I started to realize how profound Michael's statement was.

☆ ☆ ☆

Hans Bischof was about twenty-five years old when I met him through a German friend of mine. Hans moved to Coburg to work in a store selling pianos after attending a vocational school to learn all about the instrument. He could name and replace all the parts, and he could tune a piano as well. Hans also spoke almost fluent English with only a slight accent.

He was born and raised in Braunschweig in northern Germany. His mother was a cook who worked for a wealthy family, and his father was a gardener for the same family. When I met Hans, his father had passed away, but his mother was still alive and had moved to Coburg when Hans did. Hans was about 5'11" and weighed about 175 pounds. His hair was thinning, and he had a slight comb-over. He looked like a younger and thinner Pavarotti.

Soon after I met Hans, he invited me and three other people to a small dinner party at his apartment. We all arrived at the same time. I was almost embarrassed when he answered the door and invited us in. The apartment was one room, about twelve feet by ten feet. It contained a bed, a chest of drawers, and two chairs. I thought, *There isn't enough room for all of us to fit into this apartment. How are we going to have a party?*

As soon as we arrived, he set up some folding chairs in the hallway outside his apartment and left the apartment door open. He opened a bottle of wine and served each of us a glass. He then took a plate of hors d'oeuvres out of his chest of drawers. After the hors d'oeuvres, he served us the main dish, which was something he called a *Bischscoopski*. He had a hotplate on which he could fry eggs. The eggs were then laid on top of a piece of German bread that had been smeared with Velveeta cheese. He then put some ketchup on top of each egg-and-cheese sandwich and served them on individual plates. During dinner, he put on a Frank Sinatra album; and after we ate, he served German coffee and a very lovely, light pastry dessert.

As we were leaving, we all told Hans that we'd enjoyed his marvelous meal, and we complimented him on his ability to present a feast in such a small space. That was my first hint that Hans had some exceptional talents. I didn't find out until years later that he could also play the piano quite well, but that night, I learned he was an exceptionally adept and resourceful host. If we were at someone else's apartment or together in a restaurant, Hans was always the center of attention. He would get everyone involved in whatever he was doing, and it was always fun.

☆ ☆ ☆

In Germany, Ascension Thursday is also called Father's Day. The Ascension Thursday after I met Hans was an outstanding day, most of which I'll never forget. The way the Germans celebrate Father's Day in Coburg is for a group of women, usually wives and girlfriends, to prepare a wagon full of German beer for each of their men. The men gather in the marketplace and locate their wagons of beer. Someone then leads the men out of town. That particular day, Hans was the one directing all of this, which included showing each of us how to make a paper hat out of a sheet of newspaper, which we all had to wear.

About ten of us Americans joined Hans and his German friends in the parade. The march out of town took about two hours, until we arrived at a small park at the outer edge of town. The women arrived earlier and prepared a lunch for us. This was the first time we actually saw the women, because they stayed to serve us the lunch, but they never joined us. I didn't like beer, especially warm beer, but I had no choice. We were all having such a good time, thanks in great part to Hans' directions, and he demanded that we all drink our beer.

I sat for lunch with Mike and a couple of other Americans. Mike, who'd had more beers than he was used to, suggested that he and I become blood brothers. Both of Mike's parents were of Swedish descent, but only my mother was Swedish. According to Mike, that didn't qualify me to declare myself Swedish. He said I was a half-breed. What difference that made, I never quite understood, but Mike felt that if he exchanged some blood with me, I could then call myself a true Swede.

He picked up a knife off the table that was used to slice the bread and cut me across my arm. The cut wasn't deep, but it did produce a sufficient amount of blood, which was his intention. An observant woman grabbed the knife from Mike and told him that he was in no condition to perform surgery.

He laughed, and the rest of the table did as well, but I felt that we were only halfway through the required ritual that would make me a legitimate Swede.

I grabbed a fork and stabbed Mike in his left forearm. This produced more than a sufficient amount blood and a few gasps from those at the table. But Mike, ever the true Viking, took his forearm and placed my arm over his punctures, and we exchanged blood.

The rest of the day was somewhat of a blur—not only today, which is about sixty years later—but also that next day. I was told that I had a wonderful time walking back to the center of town after lunch. I somehow also made it back to the barracks because, even in my drunken stupor, I knew that I had to go to work at 4:00 p.m. I was also told that after making it back to the barracks, I passed out in my room.

Apparently, Sgt. Brown saw me passed out and knew that I was supposed to go to work. According to one witness, Brown tried to revive me by standing me up on my feet. I would smile and fall back down on the floor. He tried that twice and gave up. He ordered two guys who were also on my trick to pick me up and throw me into the back of the truck. They drove up to the hill, laid me on the ground, and left me there. They said they didn't want me throwing up in operations. I apparently laid there for about five hours before I woke up and stumbled into operations. I still had on civilian clothes, which was against the rules, and I had absolutely no idea how I got where I was. All I knew was that I was in dire need of aspirin and at least two Coca-Colas.

I found out from my friends the next day that a number of them, including Mike, had also gotten very drunk, but they didn't have to go to work. They all said that Hans drank as much or more than the rest of us, but didn't seem to be affected. Apparently, that was another one of his talents.

☆ ☆ ☆

After Dick and I decided to rent a larger apartment, we figured we could get a better deal if the apartment was in Hans' name. We all knew that rents were higher for Americans than for Germans. We also knew that a larger apartment would give Hans more room to entertain us, which he did quite often.

Our party schedule was determined by our work schedule. When we worked swings, from four in the afternoon until midnight, we couldn't party. When we worked midnights, from midnight until 8:00 in the morning, we probably *shouldn't* have partied, but we sometimes did anyway. However, when we worked days, and on the off days in between each shift, we *definitely* partied. After Father's Day, I quit drinking beer for life, but we were able to get scotch and whiskey from the Class VI store in Bamberg, and scotch became my drink of choice.

Hans was most often the host at these parties, even though he was bound to a normal work schedule, but that never came close to stopping him. He got up early every morning, cleaned the apartment, made breakfast for himself, Dick, and me, and went to work. A normal breakfast for us was coffee, fresh German rolls (*bröchen*), which were delivered daily to the house, and a soft-boiled egg for each of us. Hans prepared this before he went to work, which started at 8:00 a.m. He had these warmers that were like big mittens that would keep everything toasty for us. When Dick and I stumbled into the kitchen, about 10:00 or 11:00, everything was prepared, delicious, and warm.

One night, about 1:30 a.m., Hans and I were in a bar, and I wanted to go home, but Hans wanted one more drink. I looked at him and said, "Hans, you clod, I didn't even want the last two drinks I had. I'm going home."

Hans looked at me with a sincere look of pain in his bloodshot eyes and said, "Why did you call me a clod? I know what that means."

"I'm sorry. I was just teasing. Believe me, I'm really tired, and I do want to go home."

"But you insulted me," he said.

"We don't call that insulting; we call it teasing," I explained. "Americans do it a lot. If my father liked you, he insulted you. If he didn't like you, he ignored you."

He said, "That makes no sense. In Germany, if we like you, we compliment you. If we don't like you, we insult you."

I was going to tell him that Mark Twain once said, "You can't kid a kraut," but I figured I would then have to explain who Mark Twain was, and I was too tired.

Throughout our friendship, Hans never asked any of us for

anything and was very reluctant to accept gifts. This was not true for many of our other German friends. For some reason I never fully understood, American cigarettes were still coveted by most Germans. I was told that cigarettes were currency after the war. A German family could live almost a year on a carton of Lucky Strikes. GIs got them for free, and they could be bartered for almost anything. Why this was still true thirteen years later was a mystery to me. If any of us ran out of cigarettes in a bar, we would buy a twelve-pack of German cigarettes and smoke them. Some of us couldn't tell much difference, but there were Germans who, if you offered them an American cigarette, would take two or three and tell you they were for their wives or mothers. Hans wasn't like that. In fact, Hans didn't smoke.

One night just before I was ready to go back to the States, Hans told me that he was really going to miss me. "Maybe you can come visit me in Detroit."

He said, "I've been trying to get a visa for years."

I replied, "I didn't know that."

Hans told me that an American officer helped his parents after the war and told Hans about the U.S. He said that it had been his dream ever since—not just to visit the U.S., but to emigrate there.

"Why don't you?" I asked.

"There's a long line ahead of me."

"Is there no way to get around that?"

He said, "Yes, if an American family sponsors you."

I was surprised to hear Hans say this. I knew that he was comfortable around Americans and spoke English well enough, but I felt that he was happy with his job and planned on staying in Coburg.

"What does sponsoring a German involve? Does it take money?"

He said, "No, all you have to do is provide them a place to live for a month or so."

"Okay. I'll ask my parents if they'll sponsor you."

He looked at me for the longest while. Finally, his voice choked up as he said, "You would do that?"

I said, "I would have done it months ago, but I had no idea."

I wrote to my parents, and they investigated what it entailed. Within two weeks, they agreed to start the process. I got home in September 1960, and Hans arrived in March of 1961.

☆ ☆ ☆

I walked into the Eisdiele off of the Marktplatz, which sold Italian ice cream. My friend Pete was sitting at a small table with a German couple who looked to be a few years older than us. He asked me to join them and introduced me to the couple. The man's name was Dieter Piltz, and his wife's name was Irène.

After a few sentences in German, Irène told me that I spoke German well. She said that I sounded like I was from Norway or Denmark, which was a huge compliment. Scandinavians are known for their language skills, while the American accent is often used in movies for comic relief. Unlike the French, Germans are quick to compliment foreigners on their German, even if it isn't good. They're pleased to hear Americans, especially GIs, even try to speak their language.

At one point, Irène addressed Pete in almost perfect English. She said, "You were right, Pete, he does speak good German."

Irène spent one year in the United States as an exchange student when she was sixteen years old. When she returned to Germany, she continued her English studies and spoke almost accent-free English. Her husband, Dieter, spoke very little English. I found out that Irène was about twenty-six, and Dieter was thirty. They had a young son named Axel, and Irène was pregnant with their second child.

We had a very interesting and enjoyable conversation. As I was leaving, they asked if I'd come over on Sunday for coffee. I thought this was a casual and open-ended invitation. I responded by saying that I would.

The next Sunday, I forgot all about the invitation. I ran into Pete a couple of days later, and he told me that I'd really offended Irène and Dieter. I asked what I'd done wrong. He told me that I didn't show up for coffee on Sunday, and they had dressed up and had bought pastries and coffee just for my visit.

I asked him if he would please explain to them why I didn't show up. He said it would be better coming from me. He was going to meet them the next day for lunch and asked if I wanted to join them.

The next day, I apologized profusely, and tried to explain as best I could. Irène said to me that German invitations are much more formal than they are in the United States. She was gracious enough to say that perhaps she should have explained that to me. She asked if I were free the following Sunday, and I said yes, and I assured her I would be there, and on time.

We were taught at the Language School that if you visit Germans in their home, it's customary to bring flowers, and you should never hand the flowers to the hostess with the paper around it. When I arrived at 2:00 p.m. on Sunday, I unwrapped the flowers and put the paper in my pocket. I handed the flowers to Irène when she answered the door. I think I made a good impression.

The apartment was small, but very charming. Irène immediately brought out a pot of coffee and a tray of pastries. I didn't drink coffee, but when I was forced to, I used a lot of cream and sugar. My father told me when I was young that I'd never be a man unless I smoked Camels and drank my coffee black. I didn't like black coffee and hated Camels. By his definition, I never became a man. I immediately recognized that I had another dilemma. I was told that cream and sugar were luxuries for some families. Since they weren't present on the tray, I assumed that neither one of them used cream or sugar, so I didn't ask for it, lest I embarrass them.

For some reason or other, I never really had a sweet tooth. There were a few sweets I would eat, but most of them were called warm chocolate chip cookies. In order not to offend my hosts any more than I already had, I took a sip of coffee and then tried to kill the bitter taste by taking a bite of pastry. I managed to get through the afternoon doing that and talking as much as I could, which became easier and easier, even in German.

Dieter, Irène, and I became good friends. They were an interesting couple, and Irène wanted to have American friends in order to practice her English. Dieter liked the fact that I spoke German well enough to have political discussions with him. Being ten years older than me, he had been part of the Hitler Jugend, which was a youth group. All young (fourteen- to eighteen-year-old) German boys were encouraged to join. I was fascinated by Dieter's eyewitness account of the rise of Hitler. He had very strong opinions and didn't seem to harbor any animosity toward Americans. Coburg was never occupied by Americans, nor had it been damaged during the war. The average German in Coburg didn't have the same experience with American soldiers that most of the other Germans did.

Shortly after I met Irène, she gave birth to another son,

whom she named Olaf. That Christmas, she asked me if I'd play St. Nicholas for her children and some of the neighborhood kids. I said I didn't think I was heavy enough to play Santa Claus. She then showed me a picture of St. Nicholas, who was very thin and who visited on December 6th, not on the 25th. I showed up at the apartment early, and she gave me my St. Nicholas costume, which was primarily a black cape and a tall, pointed black hat. She then gave me a bundle of wooden switches.

"What are these for?" I asked.

She said that each child would approach me and recite a poem. They would tell me what they'd done wrong for the last year, and I was to hit them with the switch. Then I would give each kid a present.

I looked at her and exclaimed, "That's quite a bit different from our Santa Claus!"

She said, "I know it is, but it's our custom, and it's older than your custom of a jolly old fat man who gives presents."

After the first child approached me and recited his poem, I asked him what he'd done wrong, and with great trepidation, he told me all the evil sins he'd committed over the past year. When he was through, he turned around in front of me and bent over. I touched him three times with the switch. He turned his head, looked at me, and smiled.

His mother got up from the sofa, came over to me, and said, "You must hit him, and more than once."

I tried to hit him a little harder, but I couldn't do it.

Apparently, Irène explained to the German mothers that I was an inexperienced St. Nicholas, and she asked them to forgive me. I don't know whether that was a memorable Christmas for those seven children at the party, but it definitely was for me.

✩ ✩ ✩

Lt. Powers was replaced by a warrant officer whose name was Hackney. I recalled the wonderful experiences I had with Warrant Officer Wolf in Monterey, so I looked forward to meeting Mr. Hackney. Warrant Officers are able to fraternize with enlisted men. I assumed that he wouldn't be as defensive as Lt. Powers, and he could join us in the wonderful experience we all had in Coburg. Unfortunately, I dated a woman with whom he later fell in love, and ultimately married. I don't know what she told him about our relationship, which was very short, or whether it was just the fact that I'd dated her, but he quickly let me know that she was going to give me as much trouble as he could, and I should be on my toes.

By that time, I'd learned the written and unwritten rules of the Army game and was fairly confident that I could do what I wanted and still stay out of trouble. As it turned out, Hackney was also a bully, and he became as "chickenshit" as Lt. Powers. I had less than a year to go in my enlistment, and I wanted to stay in Coburg, so I put up with his antics, but I kept score.

I decided I'd get discharged in Europe, which was an option all soldiers had. That meant I'd have the opportunity to come back and visit Mr. Hackney as a civilian. I looked forward to that chance.

When our time came to be discharged, Dick also decided to take his discharge in Germany, so we were sent to Herzo Base to be mustered out of the Army. I got out on June 25th, and Dick got out on the 26th.

All soldiers learned how to count backward while awaiting their discharge. About three months before their last day, they'd yell to no one in particular, "How does eighty-nine and a wake-up sound?" which means they'd be civilians in ninety days and wanted everyone to know they were "short timers." They'd repeat that sentence almost every day, counting backward until they had about twenty days to go, at which time they shouted it to the world every day, including the wake-up day.

When that day finally arrived for me, I reported to the captain whose responsibility it was to file the papers, and follow the procedure of discharge and release. After he handed me the required papers to sign, he asked me for my Army ID card. I was going to travel around Europe for the next three months, and I knew that an Army ID card, which would allow me to shop in the PX, was a very good thing to have. I told him that I couldn't hand over my ID card, because I'd lost it.

He said, "You have to report a lost ID card immediately."

I said, "I'm reporting it now."

He looked at me for quite a long time, raised his voice, and yelled, "Are you trying to tell me you lost your ID card on the way over here?"

"Yes, sir," I answered in a calmer voice.

He said, "Teachman. I know what you're trying to do, and if I ever catch you in any PX, I'm going to throw you in the stockade."

I looked at him and said, "Sir, you would have every right to do that."

He looked at me very intensely, and I thought I might have gone too far on my very last day as a soldier. He finally said, "Specialist Fourth Class Teachman, the Army has a great deal of money invested in you. Consequently, I'm supposed to try to get you to re-enlist, but I know you well enough to say that the only way I would want you to re-enlist is on the other side. Now get the hell out of here."

I saluted him, said, "Thank you, sir," and walked out the door as a civilian.

The next day, Dick was mustered out. I strongly advised him to turn in his ID card. He and I got on the train and headed to Italy to start our new adventures. We were now transformed from GIs, who in the eyes of many Europeans were "overpaid, oversexed, and over here," into young American students who spoke fluent German.

After three weeks of travel throughout Italy, we went to the island of Capri. We stayed there a week and then took a train back to Coburg. Dick was eager to see Luzi, and I was going to be best man for Mike and Lydia's wedding. The second night I was back, I went to the bar that Warrant Officer Hackney frequented. When I walked in, I saw him sitting alone at a table in the back. As I approached him, he looked up from his beer and saw me. He didn't get up. He just sighed and asked, "What are you going to do?"

"I came here to kick the living shit out of you," I said, "but I just changed my mind. It's not that you don't deserve to have your ass kicked, but if I did, I would also be a bully. I hate bullies. So I think I'm going to buy you a drink and ask you a question."

I saw him relax, and his body language told me that he knew I was right. I ordered him a beer and asked, "Why do you act like such an asshole? Is it all about Kitty?"

He said, "It started with Kitty, but it was mostly about you. You have an attitude that says you know today is going to be great day and tomorrow is going to be even better. I haven't felt that way in years. I was determined to show you how shitty this life really is, but I never succeeded. You would look at me, and instead of anger, I could see pity in your eyes. I hated you for that."

"You must have felt that way about a lot of these guys," I said.

"I did," he said, "but you were different. No matter what I did, I never was able to get you down. You were always happy."

I got up from the table to leave and said, "I don't pity you, but I do wonder why you choose to be so unhappy most of the time. You have a good wife, you make good money, and you could enjoy life if you wanted to. It's your choice. Why you choose not to is something I just don't understand."

I paid his bar bill as I left, and I never saw him again. I later heard that he asked for a transfer to another duty station. I also heard that he and Kitty had a child. I hope that made him happy, or at least less unhappy.

☆ ☆ ☆

My time in the Army was in many ways the most free I've ever felt. This may sound ironic and even contradictory, because in this book, I've recounted my many run-ins with Army rules and restrictions. Although I fought against it, I was aware that the Army owned me most of the time. I knew that my fate for my three years of indentured servitude depended a great deal on whim, bias, and the first letter of my last name.

Although my mom and dad gave me much more latitude than my friends did, my parents were always a consideration. I had to keep in touch, and I was still their dependent. Most of the time in the Army, I was hundreds, and then thousands, of miles away from home, in the days of no cell phones. I wrote short letters reassuring them that I was still alive and not in the stockade, but otherwise, they weren't uppermost in my mind.

While I was in Germany, I made good money and had free

room and board. I drove a Mercedes, had my own apartment, and was stationed with thirty guys, most of whom were older and much wiser than me. Every eleven days, my biggest decisions were:

Where do I want to go for the next three days? Should I go to Munich or Vienna, or should I go someplace I've never been before?

During my two years in Germany, the Army gave me sixty days' vacation, and enough money to have the time of my young life.

After being discharged overseas, my mother sent me a Eurail pass, which allowed me to travel anywhere in Western Europe, first class. This allowed me to experience even more freedom than I had had in the Army. Mike talked to me about the different types of freedom when we were reading Camus. He said we all understand freedom *from* something—for example, freedom from hunger or danger. And we also understand freedom *for* something, like being able to drink at twenty-one, or in my instance, being able to drink *legally* at twenty-one. However, the kind of freedom Camus was writing about was the freedom that comes from understanding what he called "the human condition." I believe I now understand what that type of freedom means, but I've spent most of my adult life trying to accept all of what that entails.

When Mike and I talked about the freedom we experienced in the Army, he called it the ability to be capricious, which is being able and willing to act on a whim or an impulse. During my free time in the Army, between shifts and on leaves, I did what I felt like doing. Most of the time I lived in the moment, but I was also aware that I would have to go back to the Army and its rules.

CHAPTER 7

My Homecoming

During my travels in Europe, and for three months after I left the Army, I was capricious. If it were cloudy in Stockholm, I'd get on a train and end up two days later on the Riviera. I saved and borrowed enough money so that this wasn't a financial concern. I was single and on my own. The first-class trains were normally only a quarter full because they were too expensive for most Europeans. Rather than rows of seats, they had individual compartments with room for three people on each side. At night, I'd find an empty compartment, pull down the shades, and sleep until I got to my next destination. I spent ten days in Sweden and Norway, commuting back and forth from Stockholm to Oslo, which is about an eight-hour train ride each way, without ever renting a hotel room.

Soon after I came home, I enrolled at Wayne State University, lived in student housing near my parents, got married, and became a father. I never allowed myself to be capricious after that. I could never afford to be that self-centered again, as I'd never experience that kind of freedom in the years to come. After the Army, and until this day, I've had responsibilities that required me to consider the consequences for every decision I made.

I was in the Army from June 1957 until June 1960. When I entered, I was nineteen years old, and I was twenty-two when I got out. I'm now in my eighties, and I have to admit that I'm amazed, and at times amused (but also somewhat embarrassed), by my life as a soldier. My father taught me to give a man who hired me a fair day's work. I can see from what I've written that I didn't always do that. In my own defense, I can only say that I felt as if the Army didn't really care whether or not I *gave* them a fair day's work. I learned early on that hard work wasn't a criterion for promotion or recognition during peacetime.

My misadventures were not in defiance of Army rules so much as they were gambles on my part. I was prepared to pay when I lost, and I did pay—many times—but I never complained. The times that I won gave me more of what I actually joined the Army to experience.

Bob and I made a pact when we joined that we would never waste a moment. We knew when we were in a new city, in the States, or overseas, that we had an opportunity to experience something that we could never experience on our own. We took advantage of all those moments, and then some. The "and then some" cost us a couple of times, but in the long run, they were worth it.

I want to believe that had I been in the Army during wartime, I would have been a good soldier. In war, soldiers have to depend on other soldiers. I firmly believe that I would have done my best to not let my fellow soldiers down.

☆ ☆ ☆

When my three months of travel were up, I went to Coburg to say goodbye to my friends. Kerry drove me to Bremerhaven, where I took a troop ship home. He wanted to go to Copenhagen first, and I said that would be fine, because I loved Copenhagen. I'd spent three days there during my travels and would have stayed longer if time had permitted. Kerry went there to have fun and to do a business deal for his father. His dad told him that he'd bought fifty tanks from the U.S. government and wanted to sell them to the Danish government. His dad never put this in writing, but Kerry understood: Denmark was going to sell the tanks to Israel.

We arrived there in the early afternoon and checked in to a hotel. We walked around the old town for a while and then had an early dinner. We were there for only two nights, so we were eager to experience Copenhagen's nightlife, which can last until dawn. We walked into a nightclub after dinner and sat at the bar. In a very short time, Kerry's good looks, and perhaps his Austin Healey sports car that he parked right outside the door, prompted an attractive young woman to join us. She sat between Kerry and me and introduced herself in perfect English.

As was normally the case with Kerry and me, I did most of the talking, even though I knew she was only interested in Kerry. About ten minutes into the conversation, I started to think that there might be a slight chance things were going to turn out differently this time. Then a man entered the nightclub and chose to sit next to me at the bar, rather than in one of the many empty seats. My back was turned away from him when he tapped me on the shoulder and asked, "May I have a cigarette?" pointing to my pack of Winstons on the bar.

I turned toward him and said, "Sure, help yourself," and turned back to the woman to continue my conversation.

"Do you have a light?" he asked, after tapping my shoulder a second time.

I turned toward him and showed a little bit of irritation, but I lit his cigarette.

He said, "Listen, I'm not gay, but you and I are supposed to have a conversation, and if we do so, it will be much more beneficial to you than anything you might think is going to happen between you and that girl."

I looked at the guy and thought, *What the hell is going on?*

He was about my height and build, and spoke with an Australian accent. He had brown, curly hair, and almost coal-black eyes that went right through me. All the while, he smiled at me as if we were old friends. He moved to a table, and I joined him, leaving Kerry to fend for himself.

He told me who I was, just as Shula had in Paris, but he did it to establish his credentials, and then went to his main point.

"You're going to be a teacher," he said.

"No, I may have to teach for a while if I can't afford to go to law school full-time, but I'm going to be a lawyer," I said.

Then he explained, "You're an idealist. If you practiced law, it would tear you apart. Idealists need to teach. All the great men in history have been teachers—seldom in classrooms—but they were always teachers. You were born to teach. You've been gathering knowledge all of your life because it gives you a bridge to other people, and you like people. That's why you'll be a good teacher, and sometimes even a great teacher."

We (mostly he) talked for almost three hours, which was long enough for Kerry to do whatever with his newfound girlfriend. I don't remember much more than the part about being a teacher. Shula had never told me that. She said I would always be a seeker of knowledge, but didn't say anything about being a teacher.

The next day, I told Kerry about the conversation and mentioned that the reason the guy was in Copenhagen was to sell four jet planes to the Danish government, which he assumed were going to Israel. I told Kerry that he and my new friend could take credit for Israel's next victory.

The following day, Kerry drove me to Bremerhaven and my trip back to reality. The catch was, while on the ship, I'd be treated like a private in the Army. The thought of being back in the Army, even for a few days, coupled with ten horrendous days on a troop ship, forced me to seek help.

Before I mustered out, a nurse friend of mine at Herzo Base typed up an official-looking health form on Herzo Base letterhead. The letter said I suffered from acute seasickness and could not travel by troop ship. When I presented this to a captain at Bremerhaven, he said, "Almost everybody gets seasick on troop ships. What makes you different?"

I said, "My form is life threatening, according to my doctor."

He looked at me for a few moments. Kerry said I had tears in my eyes, and even *he* believed me. The captain picked up the phone and called Frankfurt Air Base. They said if I could be there by 1600 hours the next day, they would have room for me on a military transport flight.

My father had a heart attack in February 1960. My mom said that he was recovering nicely and was now doing well, but I had this terrible feeling that I was never going to see him again. On the drive from Bremerhaven to Frankfurt, Kerry's Austin Healey went into a slide on the autobahn going about ninety miles per hour. Fortunately, there were no cars next to us. The car did a 360-degree turn, but Kerry regained control and avoided a crash. It flashed through my mind that maybe my death that would prevent me from seeing my father again.

We got to Frankfurt safely with hours to spare. I thanked Kerry, and he promised to visit me in Detroit when he was discharged, which was in October. We said our goodbyes. I asked him to drive carefully on his way back.

My military transport flight left Frankfurt that afternoon and landed in Shannon Airport in Ireland later that night. It then took off the next morning for Newfoundland. About an hour into the flight, I looked out my window and couldn't see anything. The window was covered with oil. I called a WAC stewardess over and pointed to the window. She ran to the cockpit, and within minutes, we turned and headed back to Shannon.

After we landed safely, we were informed that one engine had sprung a leak, and it would be fixed shortly so that we could resume our flight. I suggested to the stewardess that it might be better to put us on another—preferably newer—plane, so they could take their time in repairing the broken engine. She said that she'd pass my suggestion along to the pilot, whom I was sure would agree with me.

To my consternation, we were on our way again in the same old, broken plane, in less than an hour. I stared out that window for the whole, eternally long flight to Newfoundland. Our stay in

Gander, Newfoundland, was about two hours. When we boarded for our last leg to Fort Dix, New Jersey, I was dismayed to find out we were on the same plane. I had to continue my vigil at the window for about five more hours.

When we landed safely in Fort Dix, I felt that I'd thwarted the gods, and I started to relax. I bought a Greyhound ticket to Detroit, boarded the bus, and took a seat near the back, where I could relax and maybe sleep. At our next stop, an attractive woman took the seat next to me. It turned out that she was part of a string trio consisting of her and her two sisters. She also sang backup on rock 'n' roll records. During our conversation, I told her of my experience in Vienna with *La Bohème*. She proceeded to softly sing "Mi Chiamo Mimi." Not only had I thwarted the gods, but I was now listening to an angel. She got out in Pittsburgh after saying goodbye, and promised to meet me again, which never happened. I moved farther back in the bus and stretched out over two seats. I was convinced that I'd be home when I woke up.

I don't know how long I was asleep when I heard a loud pounding on the bus window next to me. I sat up, and people were outside the bus yelling "Fire!" I looked toward the front of the bus, and two rows of seats ahead, a fire was blocking me from the exit. The driver was outside and told me that I could remove the window from the inside. After a few failed attempts, I finally got the window loose, and I crawled out.

The fire department arrived and put out the fire, which was caused by an overheated air conditioner. Our luggage was safe and transferred to another bus after about an hour's wait. We were about 100 miles into Ohio, and I seriously considered hitchhiking home, but it was the middle of the night.

I arrived at the Greyhound depot in downtown Detroit near dawn. I had a quick breakfast and hired a cab to take me to my parents' home on Roselawn Avenue. On the way there, I glanced at the meter and rapidly figured that the trip was going to cost me more money than I had. My homecoming was going to be sadly nostalgic for my father. He saw me arrive, and he and my mother came out to greet me.

"Welcome home," they said.

With a smile on my lips and tears in my eyes, I said, "I'm really glad to be back," and then I said, "Dad, I need $5 for the cab driver."

My Army Buddies

In this book, I've recounted most of the adventures I was looking for when I enlisted. However, it also involves another benefit that I wasn't expecting: the Army was such an intense experience, and the friendships that I formed often remained some of the deepest relationships I've ever had. I've kept in touch with some of these individuals since my time in the Army, so what follows are my memories of them:

Robert "Bob" McCall: Bob returned home from the Army just in time to re-enroll at Wayne State University for the fall semester, but his extended stay was different from mine. I was discharged on June 25, 1960, which was exactly three years after I enlisted. Bob extended his enlistment for three months in order to enjoy the summer in Germany. He didn't have the money to travel as I did, because he'd bought a brand-new VW Convertible, which he wanted to bring home. But things didn't work out the way he planned.

After Bob was discharged in September, he came back to Detroit and ultimately graduated from Wayne State University's College of Law. He practiced law for about forty years in Michigan, retired, and then moved to southwest Florida with his wife.

We've remained the closest of friends for all these years. I named my oldest son after him, and his daughter was born on my youngest son's birthday. We're in constant contact, although we don't see each other as often as we used to. I've called him often while writing this memoir to see if my memories are close enough. Most of the time, I pay attention to his comments, and some other times, I don't. After all, he's six months older than me, which makes his memories even more suspect than mine.

Don Van Stry: After the Army, Don went back to California to become a movie star. Unfortunately, that took not only talent, which he had, but also good fortune, which eluded him. He had a short marriage and eventually got a job with Universal Studios, so he *was* involved in the business, but he wasn't a star. He now lives in Carmel, California, and for the last few years, he's had a new avocation: singing and dancing in a couple of clubs in Carmel. We talk to each other periodically and visit each other less often, but we still consider ourselves the best of friends.

Don Nelowet: Don and I stayed in touch and saw one another on just two occasions after the Army: once a few years after he was married and I was newly married, and then forty years later, when I visited him on the way home from a conference in California. Don and his wife lived in Philadelphia for a while and then moved to Denver, Colorado, where they raised three children. He formed a successful business and lived an extremely good life until he recently passed away at the age of eighty-three.

Dick Pantano: Dick went home from the Army, filled out all the necessary papers, then sent for Luzi, a woman he met through Irene Peltz, and married her. Dick was and still remains one of my favorite people. They raised three sons, and after he received a degree in library science, they moved from New York City to a town in New Hampshire, where he became the head librarian at a small liberal arts college. We kept in close touch through mail and phone calls, and visited one another on numerous occasions. He passed away at the age of seventy-four from stomach cancer. I'm still in touch with Dick's family, and his youngest son has visited us in Florida and at our home in Asheville, North Carolina. I talk to Luzi four or five times each year.

Mike Holquist: Mike was my friend and mentor from the time I first met him, until his death from cancer in 2018. He graduated from the University of Illinois with a degree in Russian, and he completed his graduate work at Yale. He was the head of the Slavic Department at the University of Texas for a few years and ended his distinguished career at Yale. Mike had three sons from his first wife, Lydia, the oldest of whom is outshining his father in Russian intellectual studies at Columbia University. Mike had two more sons with his second wife, who was from Australia, and then eventually married a third wife with whom he lived during his final years as a department chairman at Yale. After his retirement, they moved to New York City, and Mike taught a few classes at Columbia right up until his passing.

Pete Warner: Pete and I weren't close friends in Germany, probably because we were never on the same trick and were only stationed together for about four months. We saw each other once in 1964. We reconnected about fifteen years ago, and now we FaceTime about three times a week. We've become the closest of friends and discuss just about every topic with only a few reminiscences about our Army days popping into the conversation. After the Army, he, too, became a much more serious student and ended up getting a PhD in economics.

He taught economics at the University of Connecticut for about six years before joining Bank of America and becoming their expert in South America. Pete lived as a young man in Rio, because his father was with the State Department, and was stationed there. Portuguese was almost Pete's native language. He also studied Russian at the Language School, learned German in Germany, and I believe studied Spanish in college.

He and his first wife divorced shortly after he took a job with Bank of America. They have two sons. After a short second marriage, he met, fell in love with, and married a Brazilian woman, who had a young son. They live in Rio, and have been happily together for the last thirty years. His two sons live in the United States: one in California and one in Connecticut with Pete's granddaughter.

David "Dave" Smith: After the Army, Dave and his wife, Rosi, moved to Des Plaines, Illinois. Dave finished his Master's and started teaching Spanish at the high school level, which he did until he retired. He and Rosi have two girls and a few grandchildren. They visit Rosi's hometown of Coburg on a regular basis, and have done so for the last fifty years. Dave and I talk on the phone, although not as frequently as I do with Pete and Don, but we never have trouble continuing our conversations, which are mostly extensions of our time together in the Army. Dave visited me once in Detroit in about 1969 and spent the day with me in the inner-city high school where I was teaching history. He remarked that my daily routine was considerably different from anything he'd ever experienced in Des Plaines.

Hans Bischof: My parents sponsored Hans to come to this country. He arrived in Detroit in 1961 and spent two months living with my family. He knew a German family in Chicago who got him a job there, which eventually led to him becoming an executive (and a legend) with Yamaha International. He opened their first American operation in San Francisco, and less than five years later, at Yamaha's first European venture in Hamburg, Germany. In less than five years, Hans went from being a piano salesman in a Chicago department store to the head of Yamaha Europe.

I visited Hans a couple of times in Germany, and he visited me a few times in the U.S. In recent years, we've lost track of one another.

When I came home from the Army in 1960, I immediately enrolled in college and finished my BA degree and my Master of Arts in teaching in three years. I was a much more serious student after the Army, and my grades qualified me for entrance into the doctoral program in philosophy of education. I finished the required classes for my doctorate in two years and passed my oral exams. My dissertation and final degree took a little longer and was much more tedious, but I did receive my PhD. By the time I'd finished my Master's, I realized that I wanted to be a teacher for the rest of my life.

My Master's degree gave me a significantly higher wage, whereas my PhD only resulted in a small bump in salary, as there aren't many teachers in high schools with a PhD. I actually didn't intend to finish my dissertation until I was offered the opportunity to teach at Wayne State University part-time, but I was told that first I had to clear up a couple of issues.

The government reinstated the G.I. Bill in 1966. It was retroactive to 1955, which meant that I had four years of eligibility. I was making $5,000 a year as a teacher and worked two evenings and weekends to make ends meet. The G.I. Bill afforded me more than $400 a month, as long as I was enrolled full-time. I finished my required classes in philosophy for my PhD and for my cognate field, which was psychology. I even took a number of classes I always wanted to study, such as religion, art, and music, which my adviser classified as "directed study." I enrolled in all these classes and attended them faithfully, because I liked the subjects and/or the professors. I passed the tests with high grades, and I wrote the required papers in longhand, but I didn't turn all of them in because they had to be typed, and I couldn't type. So I took "incompletes" in three of my classes, which allowed me a year or two to finish the classes and get a grade. I had to remove those incompletes in order to teach at the university, which I did by hiring a typist.

I also started working seriously on my dissertation. The process went smoothly until I ran into problems with the dissertation committee—specifically, with one member of that committee. He'd approved my dissertation without fully reading it, and when he *did* read it, the weekend prior to my oral defense, he decided that it was a racist document. He told my adviser that he wanted me to change my thesis completely. My adviser, who at that time was getting ready to retire, suffered a nervous breakdown, which delayed me from getting final approval for my dissertation for almost two years.

I taught in secondary schools for thirty-three years, the last eight of which I was the Social Studies Department chairman, and I was an adjunct professor for forty-seven years. I taught in two wealthy suburbs of Detroit and spent eleven years in an inner-city school in Detroit. I was also a consultant for the State of Michigan Board of Education for twelve years. I loved teaching and recently wrote a book about my experiences, which I self-published.

A buddy of mine once called me an "easy" friend. I asked him what that meant, and he told me, "There are easy friends and difficult friends. You never have to lie to an easy friend. If he drops by and you're not in the mood, you can tell him that, and he won't be offended. If you're meeting someone else for a drink and he asks you what you're doing after work, you can tell him the truth. Difficult friends are sometimes offended by the truth, so in order not to hurt them, you have to make something up."

From then on, I adopted his position. I have easy friends and I have difficult friends. I enjoy, respect, and in my own way, love them all. However, I never have to make excuses to my easy friends. They make few, if any, demands. Difficult friends require more maintenance.

I've kept those two categories of friends for many years. But my memories of my friends in the Army caused me to add a new category. Today, I still have easy friends and difficult friends, but I also have Army buddies... who are in a class by themselves.

About the Author

Gerry Teachman and his wife, Mary Jean, reside in Juno Beach, Florida, during the winters, and in Asheville, North Carolina, during the summers. They were both born and raised in Detroit, Michigan, where Gerry taught in three high schools in and around Detroit for twenty years. He was asked to be a consultant for the Michigan Department of Education for twelve years, and was an adjunct professor at Wayne State University in Detroit for forty-seven years. He wrote a book about his experiences as an educator called, *Tales Out of School: Told by a Teacher*, which is available through Amazon.

CPSIA information can be obtained
at www.ICGtesting.com
Printed in the USA
JSHW041921181022
31825JS00001B/90